REPUBLICANS

SPECIAL THANKS TO JANE GOULD,
FOR HER KEEN EYE, DRY WIT, AND FOR NOT LETTING US SAY ANYTHING
WITHOUT THOROUGHLY VALIDATING FACTS AND SOURCES.

# REPUGLICANS

Published by BOOM! Town, an imprint of BOOM! Studios.

FIRST EDITION

Book design by Michael Kellner

A catalog record for this book is available from OCLC and on our website www.boom-studios.com on the Librarians page.

For information regarding the CPSIA on this printed material call: 203-595-3636 and provide reference # EAST   65951

# REPUGLICANS

## ART BY
PETE VON SHOLLY

## COMMENTARY BY
STEVE TATHAM

BOOM!
TOWN

# INTRODUCTION

APPARENTLY you *can* judge a book by its cover. When the press release for "The Repuglicans" was released in February of 2010, right-wing blogs lit up with criticism of the book. Not a single page or word of the book was released — just the cover. It was called "stupid," "unoriginal," "juvenile," "infantile," "lame," "cowardly," "a monstrosity," "horrible," "ignorant," "dumb," and "tiresome," among other things. Now, I'm not saying that it isn't all those things; I'm just saying those criticisms were lucky guesses. No one knew what was depicted or written on its pages.

Howls went up that the book isn't as edgy, subversive, or rebellious as it aspires to be. That it is controversial for controversy's sake. The question was asked whether this is the best The Left has to offer. God, let's hope not, or political discourse is dead. This book is not edgy, subversive, or the official statement of any ideology or party. It's two guys cracking wise. I have a few health tips while I'm making pronouncements. If this is the kind of book that's gonna make you upset, I would urge you not to buy it...or even talk about it on your keenly insightful political blog. Problem solved. Seems obvious enough. If you're allergic to peanuts, don't eat Snickers. Another thing that's bad for you: don't make up stuff that's not in a book you've never read and argue against the things that are not in it. That's really liable to stress you out. And a little crazy.

So what is a "Repuglican"? First of all, it is not synonymous with "Republican." There are 55 million Republicans in the United States. Most of them are decent, honorable people. The Republican limited government, state's rights, traditional American values, pro-business political philosophy is a reasonable and worthwhile set of beliefs. Real Republicans and real Democrats share a common goal: they want the United States of America to be a better place for all its people. The Republican party has its fair share of towering intellects and inspiring heroes. None of them are described in the pages that follow.

There are 61 people in this book. Most of them are Republicans. Some are not. While not all of them are vampires as far as we know, all of them are deeply unpleasant in some manner or fashion. Lou Dobbs, Glenn Beck, and Bill O'Reilly claim to be independent. Fine. They are still Repuglicans. A Repuglican is someone who espouses conservative ideology to serve his or her own personal agenda without concern for the greater public good. A Repuglican knowingly manipulates the public, whipping them into a frenzy through not entirely true statements, in order to further his or her own career. This, as you might already realize, is not helpful. Poet Richard Armour summed it up when he said, politics, for "all too long, has been concerned with right or left instead of right or wrong."

STEVE TATHAM

*Now over to Pete:*

    he said.
Although I started this "project" by entertaining myself making funny pictures of people I didn't like and therefore got top billing, Steve gets to talk first because he has a tie.
Anyway, here's the thing:
Believe it or not, I don't have anything against conservatives or Republicans or "tea partyers" (as long as they don't wear funny hats and dress up like minutemen and carry horrible pictures of concentration camp victims with OBAMACARE plastered above them and have assault rifles slung over their shoulders at public rallies...) *per se.* But it doesn't work for me to just say, "Well, all politicians are equally bad so you can't just criticize one group, etc." As an artist and an American and a human being I see some UNPRECEDENTED BULLSHIT going down against our President, who I happen to like. Say what you will, he never took the low road and talked shit about his enemies in public. Like they all did. And do. Some people will say ANYTHING in their frothing frenzy of freak out, no matter how insane. (Palin doesn't like somebody using the word "retarded" and trots out her phony outrage... but she stood at podiums during the presidential campaign chanting "Who is Barack Obama?" while her screaming shills screeched "Terrorist! Kill him!" and that was okay??? And now she says name-calling is bad and hurtful. Boo fucking hoo.)
Shouldn't we get upset when our president wants to give kids a little pep talk about staying in school and getting an education and how education is good and important—and that's all he wants to do—and suddenly the situation is twisted into one where he's supposed to be just like Saddam Hussein or Kim Jong Ill, that we are living in a socialist fascist un-American dictatorship and... and that they... *they're* trying to take away our FREEDOM!!!... so you better not let your kids go to school that day because they might, I don't know, *hear* something....We should stand up and call that bullshit, ALL of us! Or at least draw some fangs on a picture of a conservatard!
    That's the kind crap I'm pissed off about. (And yes, maybe one or two Democrats also suck a little. There.)

# REPUGLICANS

ROGER AILES created the Willie Horton ad for George Bush Sr. that used a deliciously potent combination of racism and fear to help the Old Man win the presidency over Michael Dukakis. Ailes, to be fair, does have scruples. He wrestled over one question regarding the ad. He said "the only question is whether we depict Willie Horton with a knife in his hand or without it." Ailes worked for such Repuglicans as Ronald Reagan, Rush Limbaugh, and Richard Nixon. When Murdoch was beginning to get Fox News off the ground in 1996, he could think of no one better to run the day-to-day operations than Roger. Mr. Ailes continues to oversee the channel, churning out lunatic ranters and Fembot propaganda hostesses. But there's trouble in paradise. There are two camps within News Corp, the company that owns Fox News. There are the fans of Ailes, the bellowing, bulbous, balloon-faced blowhard we know and love. And then there are those that respect journalism, like Murdoch's son-in-law, who said the whole family is "ashamed and sickened" by Ailes. Wanna know who wins? Follow the money.

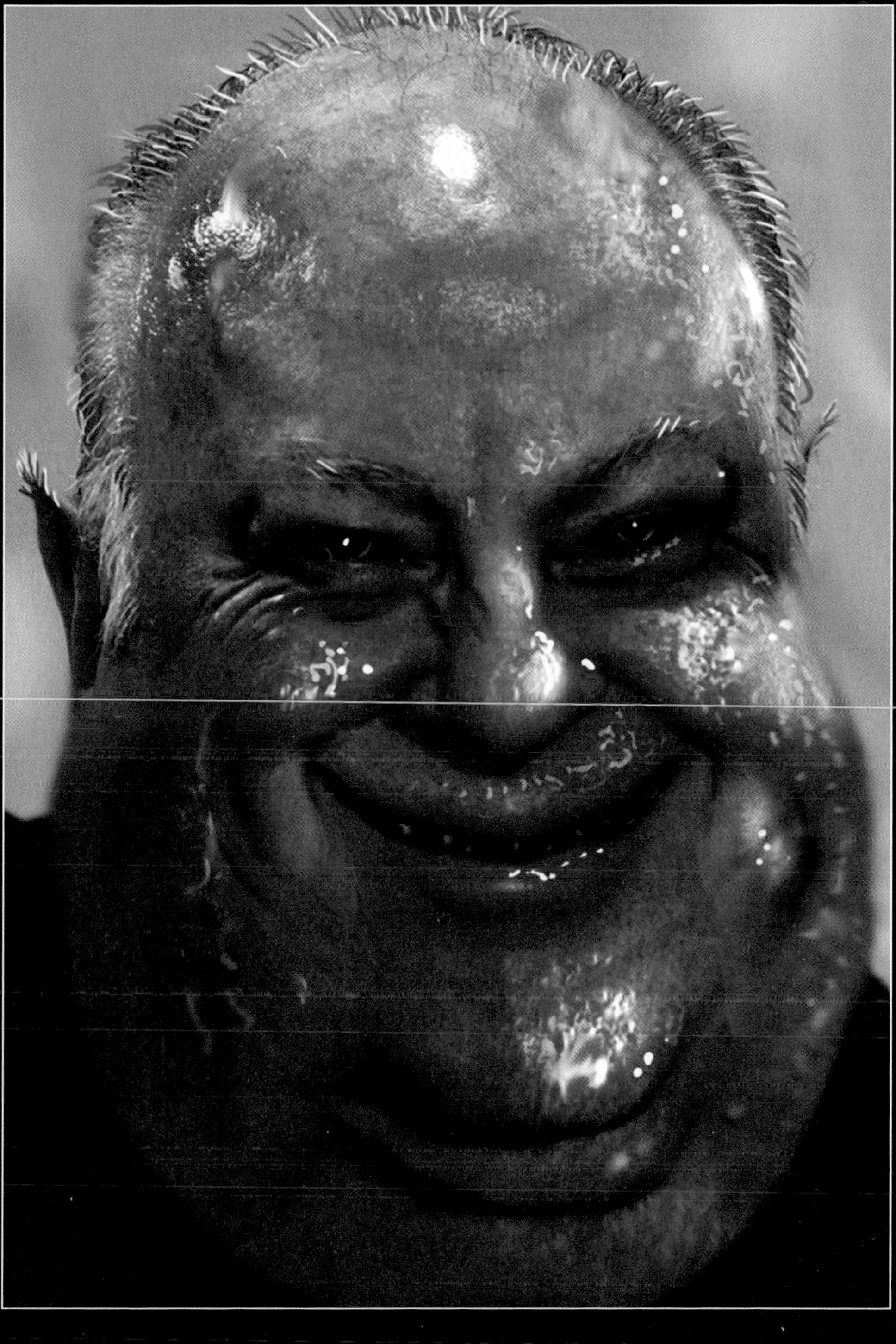

"DICK ARMEY" might be a good name for troops whose sole mission seems to be drawing unstable people from the dark corners of the earth by promising the crazier they are, the more likely they'll get on TV. But while the army of people who enjoy scrawling misspelled insults on signs featuring the President may be lead by a graceless former Texas congressman named "Dick Armey," they call themselves "FreedomWorks." Ironically, Armey, for the bulk of his life, has enjoyed the benefits of government-provided health care as a politician and a professor. Yet he has made it his focus to deny this benefit to his fellow citizens. What prepared him for this moment? You remember. He partnered with Newt Gingrich to lead a revolution and fight people like liberal, openly gay Congressman Barney Frank, whom Armey nicknamed "Barney Fag." Together, they tried to destroy Social Security. Dick said that if that didn't work out, he could always make boatloads of money being a cigarette and drug company lobbyist. Once that came to pass, he decided to use his wealth to disrupt public meetings. It's civil disobedience without the civility. You can recognize him by the bottom-feeding sludge between his teeth.

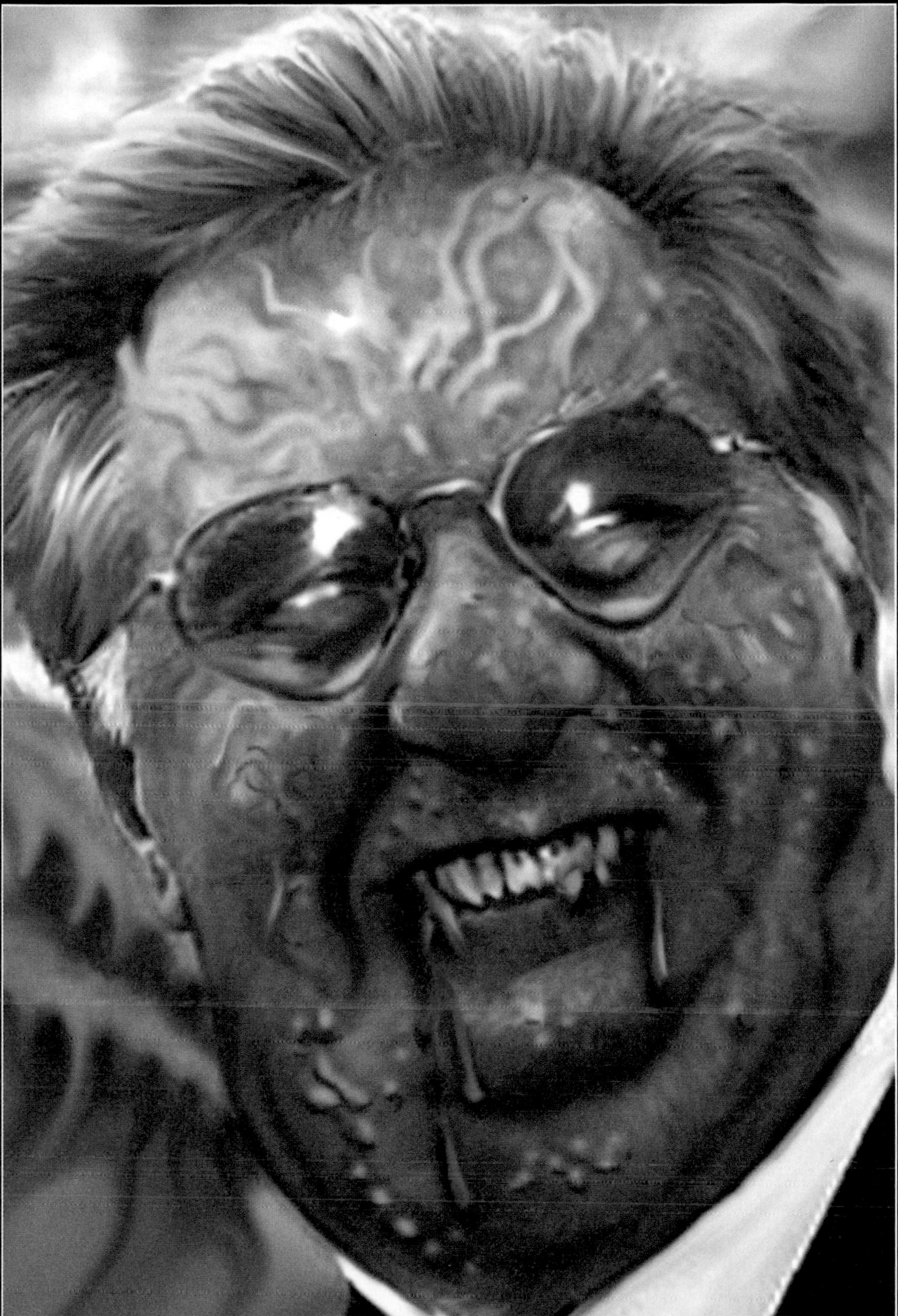

THERE ISN'T ENOUGH LITHIUM on Earth to help poor Congresswoman Bachmann (R-MN). The best way to even begin to understand the vast landscape of her undiagnosed mental illness is to read her own words:

- "It's part of Satan, I think, to say [homosexuality] is gay. It's anything but gay."
- "Literally, if we took away the minimum wage—if conceivably it was gone—we could potentially virtually wipe out unemployment completely because we would be able to offer jobs at whatever level."
- "To believe in evolution is almost like a following; a cult following."
- The mortgage crisis was caused by "loans made on the basis of race and little else."
- She questions if Obama "is secretly in favor of getting rid of the dollar and replacing it with a multi-national currency."
- "The global warming hoax. It's all voodoo, nonsense, hokum, a hoax."
- "Carbon dioxide is natural. It is not harmful. It is part of Earth's life cycle."
- She believes Obama is also "orchestrating a conspiracy involving the Census Bureau."
- And lastly, she says of the Obama administration: "These people are not connected to reality."

Good people of Minnesota's 6th District, run for the hills!

# MICHELE BACHMANN

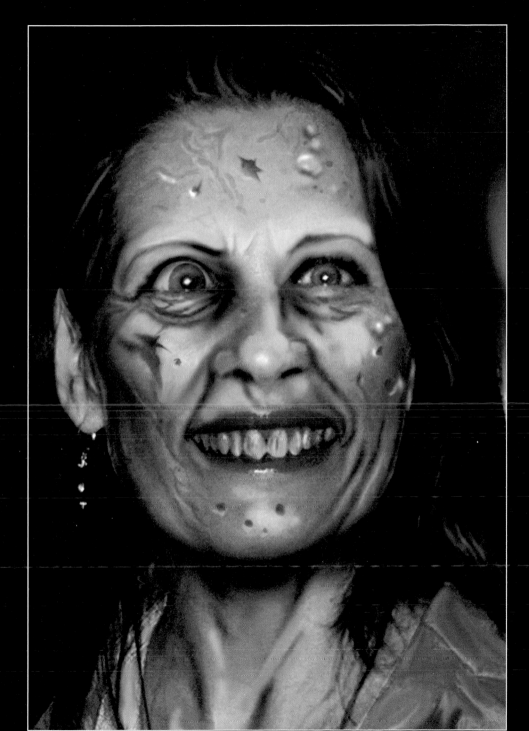

HAVE WE LEARNED NOTHING from the works of Ricky Martin? Well, Glenn Beck has, dammit! He was getting jiggy with "Livin' La Vida Loca" in the '90s because that's when he was a Top-40 DJ. And that, ladies and gentlemen, is the only training in journalism or world affairs the man has. College dropout and recovering drug addict, Beck says "I consider myself a libertarian." Yet everyone else considers him an idiot. Albeit, an idiot who's getting $23 million dollars a year to cry like a baby on TV and say moronic things like Barack Obama is reforming health care as "reparations for slavery." Beck started something called the 9/12 Project because he's nostalgic for the day after the September 11, 2001 terrorist attacks when, according to him, America was less partisan and more united. He celebrates this unity by instigating his followers to go to Tea Party rallies and hold up pictures of President Obama decorated with Hitler moustaches. And, of the 9/11 victims, he has said, "When I see a 9/11 victim family on television, or whatever, I'm just like, 'Oh, shut up.' I'm so sick of them because they're always complaining." Clearly, zombies have eaten his brain.

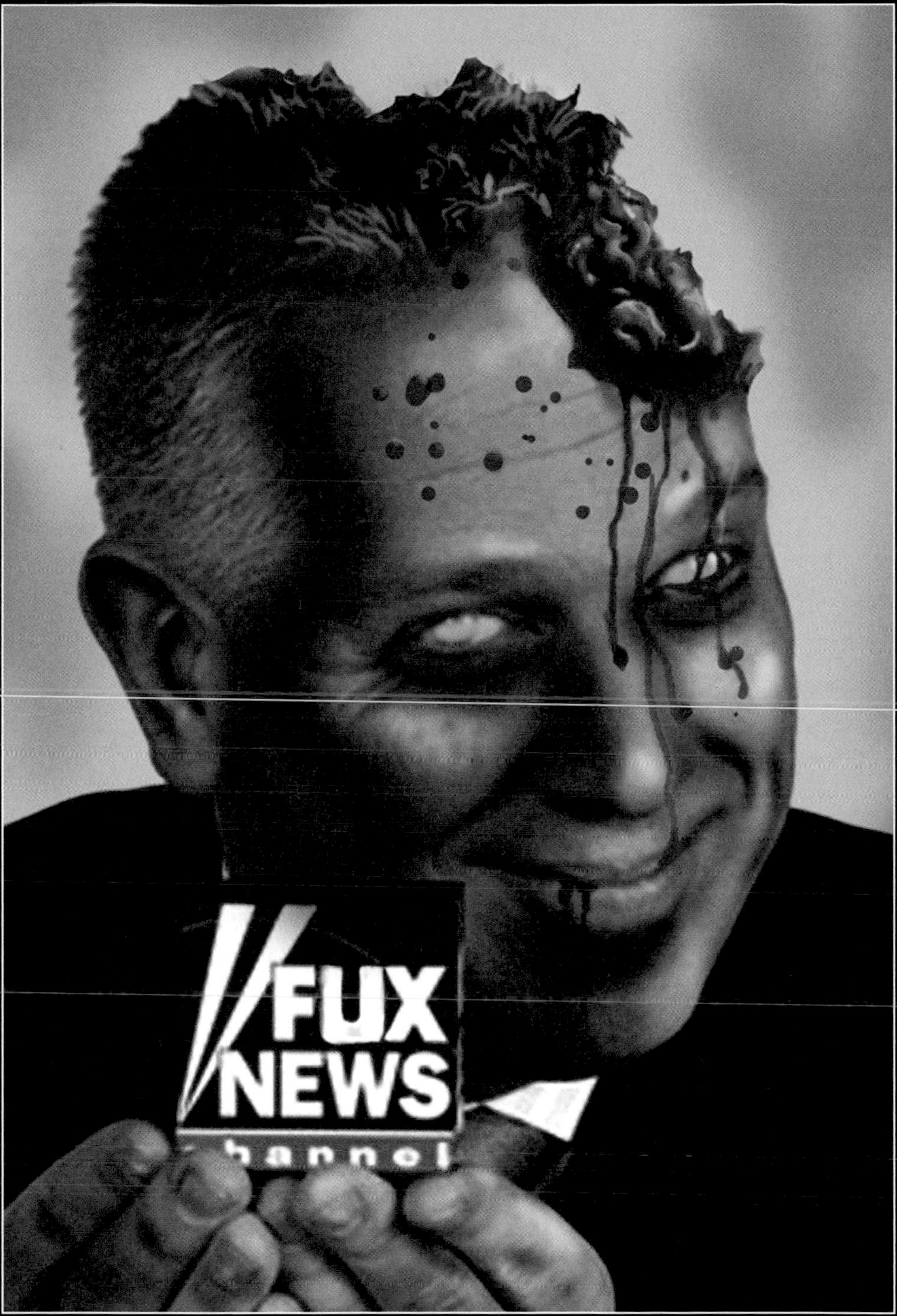
FUX
NEWS
channel

PEOPLE LIKE ROY BLUNT take pro-family stances (not to be confused with Larry Craig's "wide stance"). Never mind that no one is anti-family. They profess being proud to be an American, forgetting people on every point of the political spectrum are proud of their country. They are "pro-life," as opposed to the non-existent "pro-death" crowd. They incite the public with statements like, "What I don't know is why the president can't produce a birth certificate. I don't know anybody else who can't produce one. I think that's a legitimate question." Compounding the problem is an astonishing lack of understanding regarding what should be common sense, such as when Mr. Blunt states that an uninsured American can get a hip replacement "if they go to the emergency room. I think they can get that done." Uh, no, they can't. Some politicians love to spend money they don't have and criticize others for doing the same. They cut taxes for the rich during wartime and expect the poor to pay for it. They shill for big oil and give no-bid government contracts to Halliburton. There's a word for someone who tries to obfuscate when his job is to clarify. That word, ironically, is "Blunt."

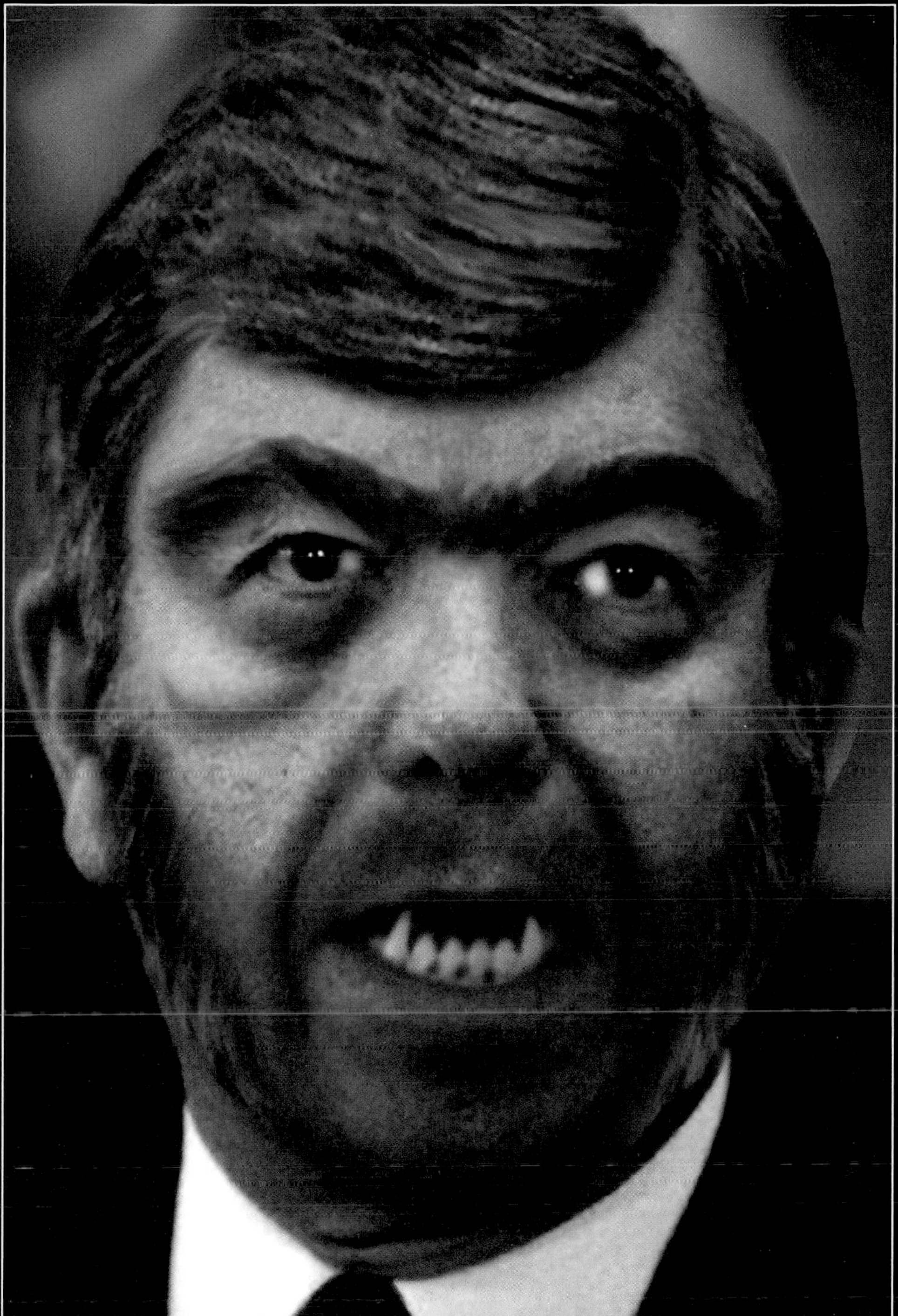

AS ONE of the senior members of the GOP leadership in the House of Representatives, Boehner is a man who knows how to get things done. An example, you ask? Okay, before a vote on important legislation affecting the tobacco industry, John wisely used his time on the House floor to pass out checks to various Congressmen. Checks, you say? What kind of checks? From the tobacco lobby, of course. Now there's a "can-do!" attitude. And totally transparent. No backroom deals for him; he just waltzed around the room, passing out money. If only his Democratic opponents could learn from the House Minority Leader, maybe they'd actually get some shit done instead of wasting all their time arguing over policy and what's best for the country. Put the cash on the barrelhead, baby, and get down to business. It may seem like he's one of the living dead, but that's how to make it happen. Thanks for leading the way, Congressman. This is the guy who called health care reform "the greatest threat to freedom I have seen." Really? C'mon, Congressman, you don't have to look too far to see a greater one. Check a mirror.

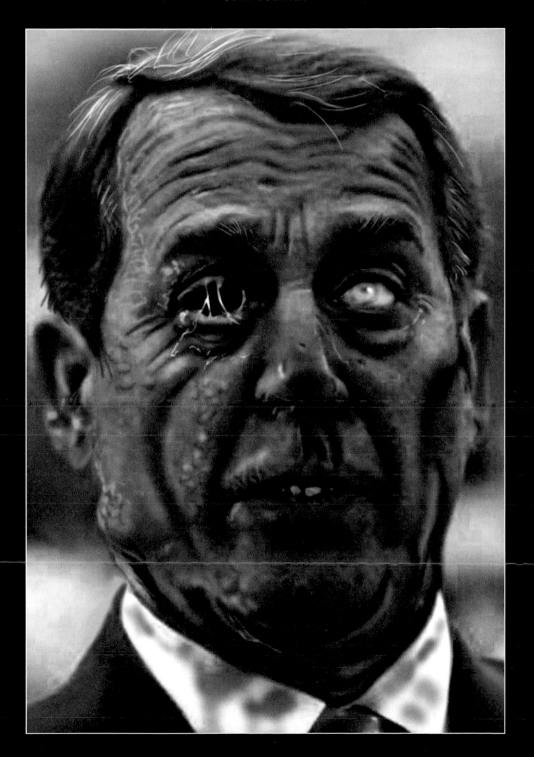

I THINK WE CAN ALL AGREE that Barack Obama is not Adolf Hitler. Furthermore, I think it's fair to say that the President of the United States has not used a Gestapo-like security force to impose a Marxist dictatorship. And empirical evidence suggests that he has not taken away anybody's guns and, in fact, there are significantly more firearms in the United States now than when he took office. If all this seems relatively obvious to you, then perhaps you are a sane person subject to the constraints of facts and reason. That would mean you are not the congressman from the 10th district of Georgia, Paul Braun. One wonders when he says things like, "You have to remember that Adolf Hitler was elected in a democratic Germany" when discussing the President, why he still has a job. And, when he says of Obama's policy for national service, "That's exactly what Hitler did in Nazi Germany," one might also wonder why every time he opens his mouth, his pants don't immediately explode into flames. Followed by his head.

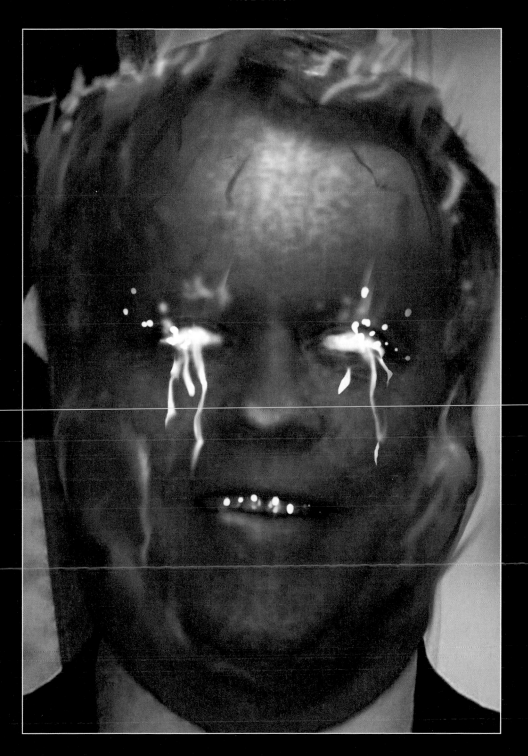

HE'S LIKE YOUR GRANDPA when he hasn't had a bowel movement in a really long time and he's all balled up in anger. He's Pat Buchanan! Crotchety and defiant, his insides are lined with vitriol. When he ran for President in 1996 (and when didn't he run for President, really?), he came out swinging with incendiary rants about leading bands of peasants with pitchforks against the establishment. He drew adulation from neo-Nazis, archconservatives, and religious zealots far and wide. There's nothing "neo" about his conservatism; he's a Paleo-Conservative. A graduate of the Nixon White House School of Dirty Tricks, he graduated Magna Cum Douche when the fame and fortune of writing a column came calling. Buchanan refers to multiculturalism as "an across-the-board assault on our Anglo-American heritage." He likes to call himself a "European-American," which is his way of reminding you of his guiding principle that "our culture is superior because our religion is Christianity and that is the truth that makes men free." Free indeed. Free to say things about Adolf Hitler, like Hitler, was "an individual of great courage, a soldier's soldier in the Great War, a political organizer of the first rank." God bless freedom.

PAT BUCHANAN

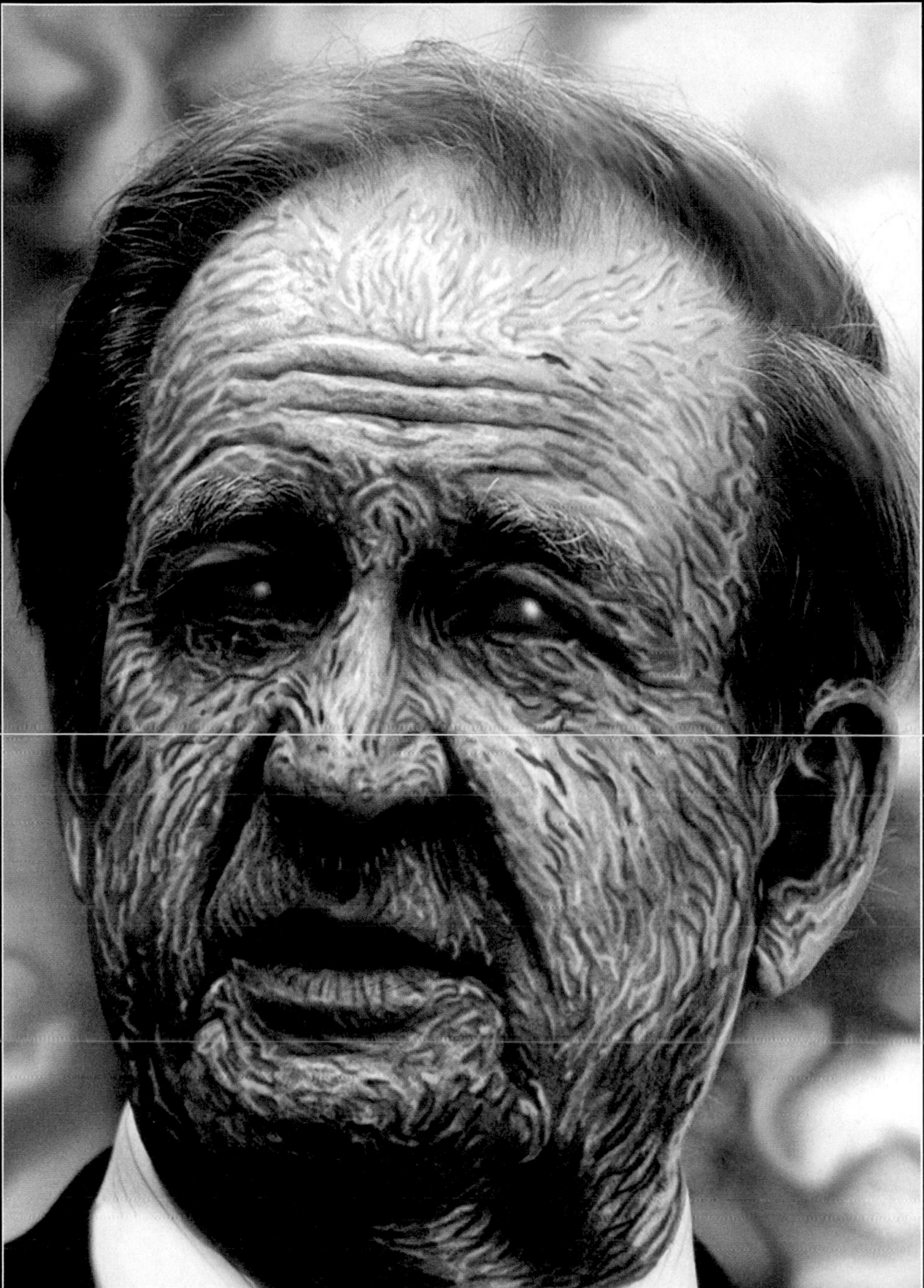

THOUGH HE MAY SEEM like he just crawled out from under a bridge, this Connecticut-born (what gives with the ginormous cowboy belt buckles?) son of a President had just a little leg up in life. With money left over from his education trust fund, he started an oil company called Arbusto that went el busto. I know you were going to do that with your leftover trust fund money. He then invested in the Texas Rangers, triggering a Securities and Exchange Commission investigation. This prepared him, of course, to be governor of Texas and leader of the free world, where he presided over the crack security team that allowed the terrorist attacks of September 11, 2001 to occur. Though Bush had already sent the economy straight into the toilet, the good people of the United States put American flag stickers on their cars and rallied behind the only president they had. However, his inability to form coherent sentences and limited understanding of the world around him continued to raise great suspicion. Not the brightest man to ever serve in the White House, even as President, he initially thought "Iraq" was a phrase used to begin a game of pool.

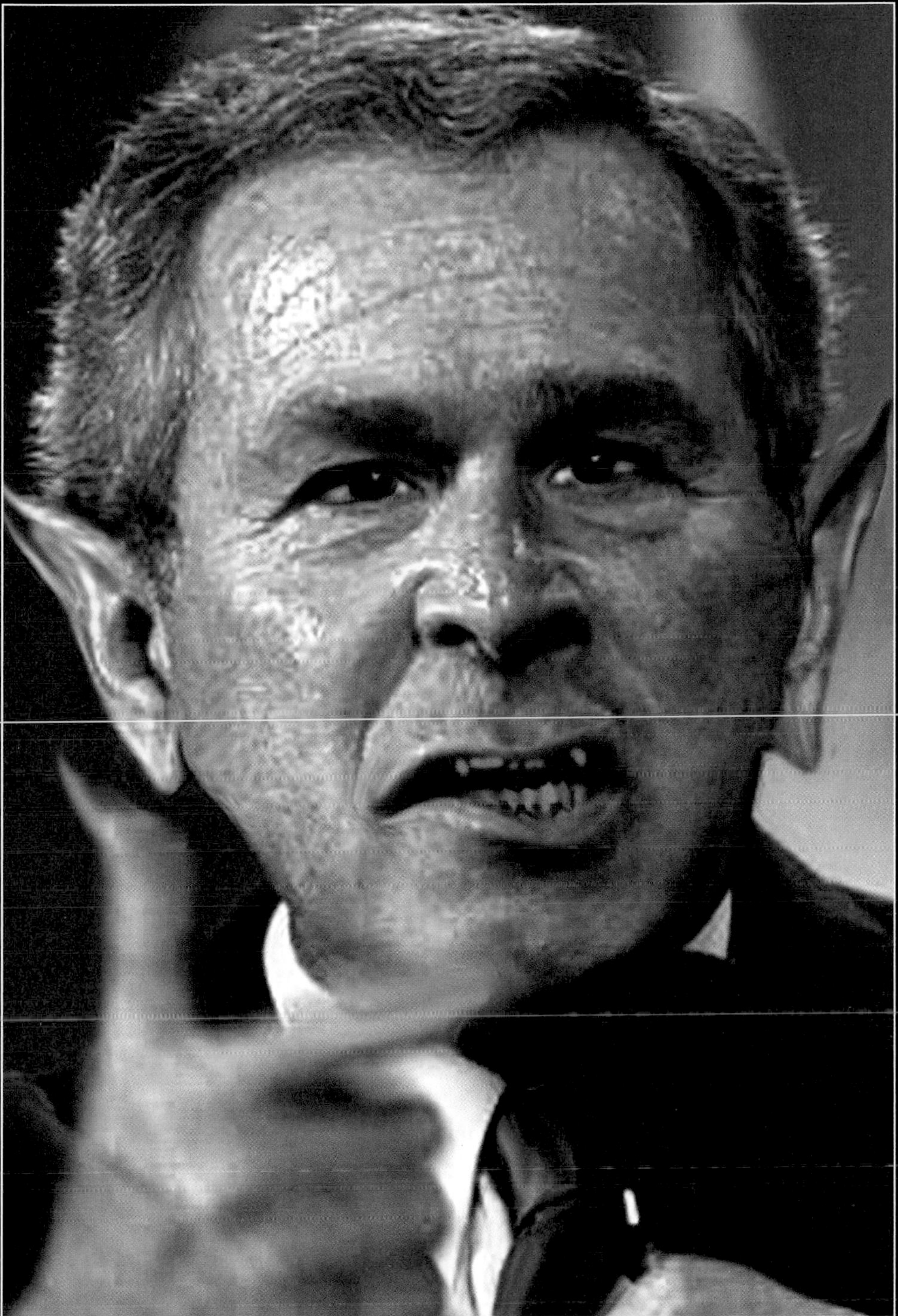

CONGRESSMAN CANTOR suggests the President owes an apology to Fox News for questioning their biases. Here's a common tactic used on Fox News: the host begins a sentence with "some people say..." then continues by saying the most outlandish accusation the writers can dream up. It's not an accusation, it's simply reporting "what some people say." Who are these people? That's not stated, but I think you know who they are. People in the Fox News newsroom. That makes researching what "some people say" a breeze. One trip to the water cooler and your work is done. Let's try it, shall we? Some people say Eric Cantor is the biggest douche in the House of Representatives. The GOP's #2 congressman cozies up to the Birther Movement and any nut job's rant against President Obama. Some say Cantor looks to Rush Limbaugh for ideas on how to fix the economy. Oh wait, that wasn't "somebody." Cantor himself said that. But some people do say he's so opposed to the economy improving under Obama that he describes the Recovery Act, which has created 2 million jobs, as having "failed miserably." Wasn't that fun? Now you're ready to go work at Fox News.

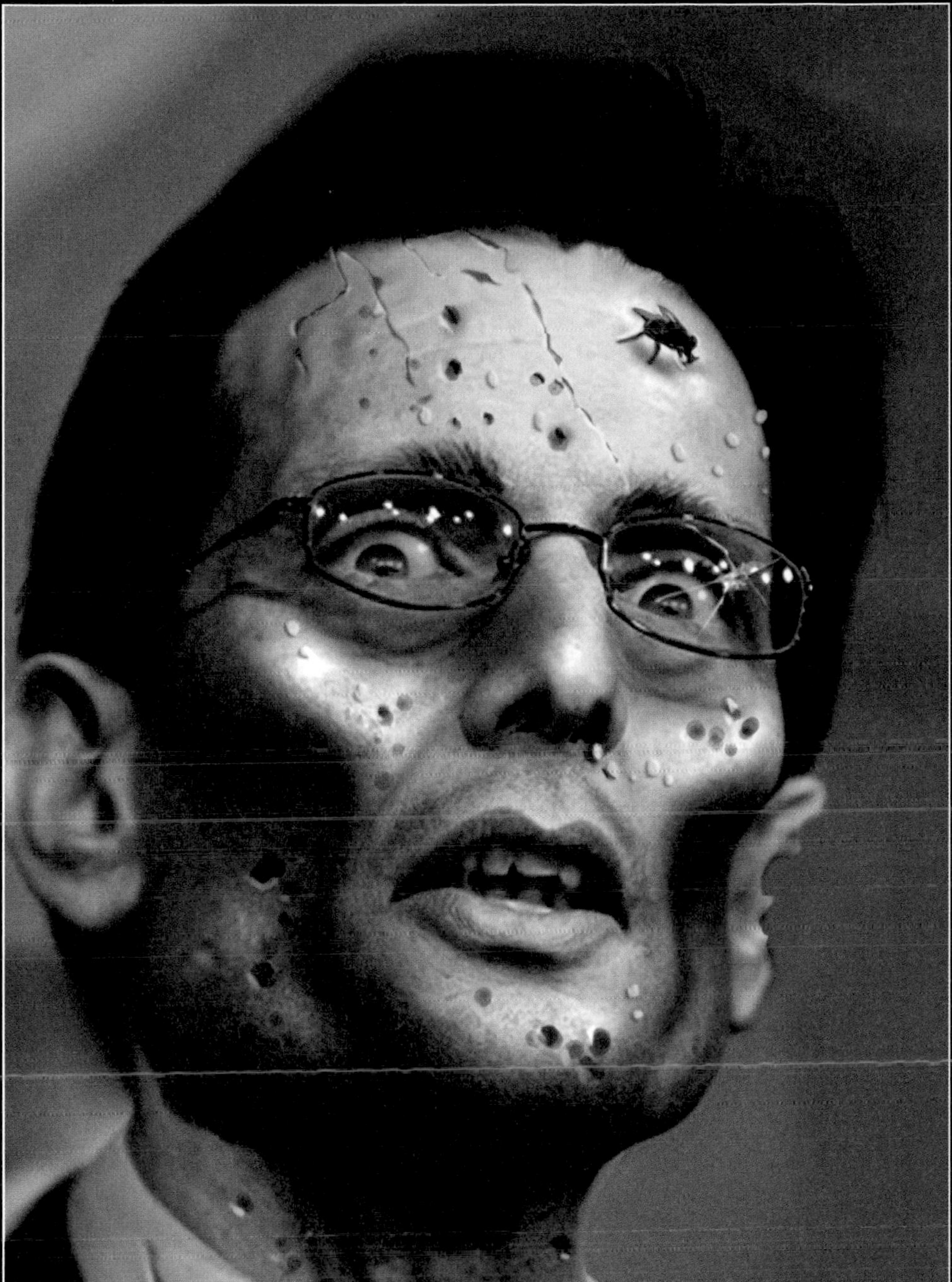

DICK CHENEY was George Bush Sr.'s Chief of Staff. Foresight on the Old Man's part. He knew if he could get his son into the White House then certainly he'd need a nanny. If not a nanny, then someone who could actually be the real president...or, at the very least, a drinking buddy. Bush Jr. and Cheney formed a close bond and did, in fact, very much enjoy partaking in alcohol together. Dick was arrested for driving under the influence twice, and George once; an all-time record for a President and Vice President. While waiting around to secretly rule the world, Cheney ran a company called Halliburton that fights wars for money. In his spare time, while Vice President, Cheney enjoyed getting drunk and shooting people in the face. Since leaving office, he must spend much of his time wearing one of those beer hats filled with venom because, suddenly, he has nothing nice to say about his country. As a result of his many heart attacks, it is thought that his heart is made up of mechanical spare bits, and there is speculation that, in fact, the only human part left in his entire body is the sneer.

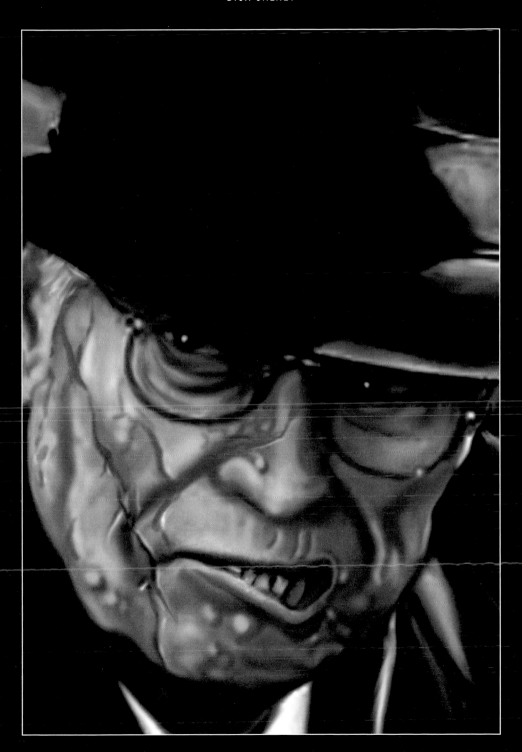

SWIFT BOAT VETERANS FOR TRUTH, the anti-John Kerry group, had about as much to do with swift boats, veterans, or truth as Octomom has to do with restraint. Jerome Corsi, who funded the group, also wrote a book about Kerry called *Unfit for Command*. Clearly he has a man-crush on John Kerry, because he just can't stop talking about him. The book was a huge hit, which is startling because who knew his fans could read? Perhaps they liked the cover. The sequel was a book he wrote four years later. It is a fairy tale about Barack Obama called *The Obama Nation*. To put a finer point on it, a Los Angeles Times reviewer had this to say about the book's message: "You can pretty well sum the whole thing up this way. 'The Democratic candidate is a deceitful jihadist drug addict who, if elected, plans to impose a black supremacist, socialist regime.'" Yada, yada, yada... you can hear that story anytime you're trapped on a desolate highway with only road-kill and AM talk radio to keep you company (good luck distinguishing the two).

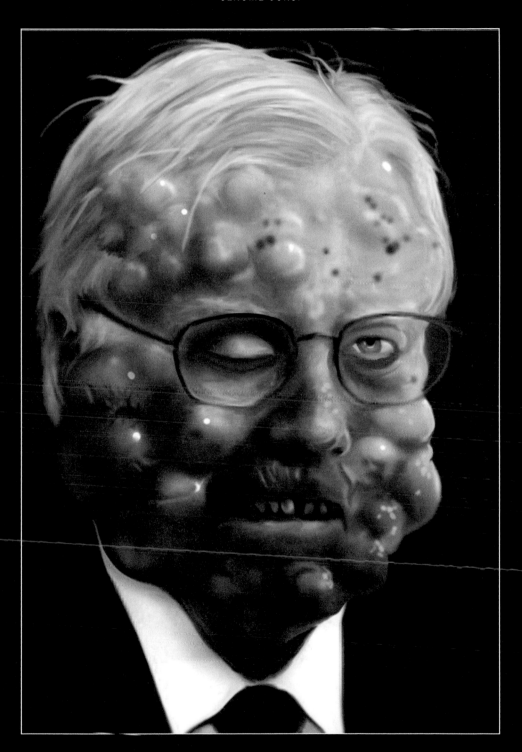

A WOMAN whose mouth needs to be washed out with chloroform, this professional provocateur will say anything to get invited on cable television talk shows. She is known for such bons mots as when she said of 9/11 widows, "I have never seen people enjoying their husbands' deaths so much." She also endeared herself to America when she hissed about Vice President Al Gore and California Governor Gray Davis: "Both were veterans, after a fashion, of Vietnam, which would make a Gore-Davis Presidential ticket the only compelling argument yet in favor of friendly fire." Not only that, Ann has been caught engaging in voter fraud and publicly lying about her age. One is hard-pressed to blame her for her uncivilized behavior, since she is thought to be an alien life form from a nebula far away. She could never get the story straight because, in fact, she's estimated to be 14 centuries old in Earth years.

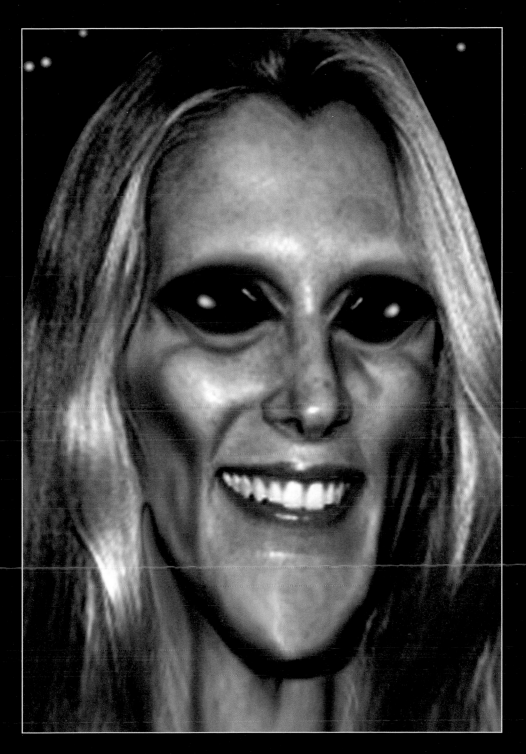

NOT THAT THERE'S ANYTHING WRONG with it, but Florida Governor Charlie Crist has been denying rumors of his gayness for years. Many insist he's not just a little "Miami metrosexual" but Barbara Streisand's "Funny Girl: The Original Soundtrack Recording," transsexual vampire gay. After decades of being a "confirmed bachelor," he fell in love, just in time for John McCain to select Chuck as his running mate. The question is, did he fall in love with power or with Carol Rome, the woman he hurriedly married? She has a business selling Halloween costumes. The irony is, she sells fake beards and she may be one too. Sadly, despite his image makeover, he didn't get picked as McCain's running mate. Now he has to sleep with a woman by law. Okay, the law doesn't say they have to sleep together, but it does say they are married and the law also says it's illegal for him to marry a man in Florida. See, that's the point. Not that he hates himself so much he may be pretending to be what he's not, but that his self-hatred leads him to oppose gay marriage, gay adoption and civil rights for people like himself.

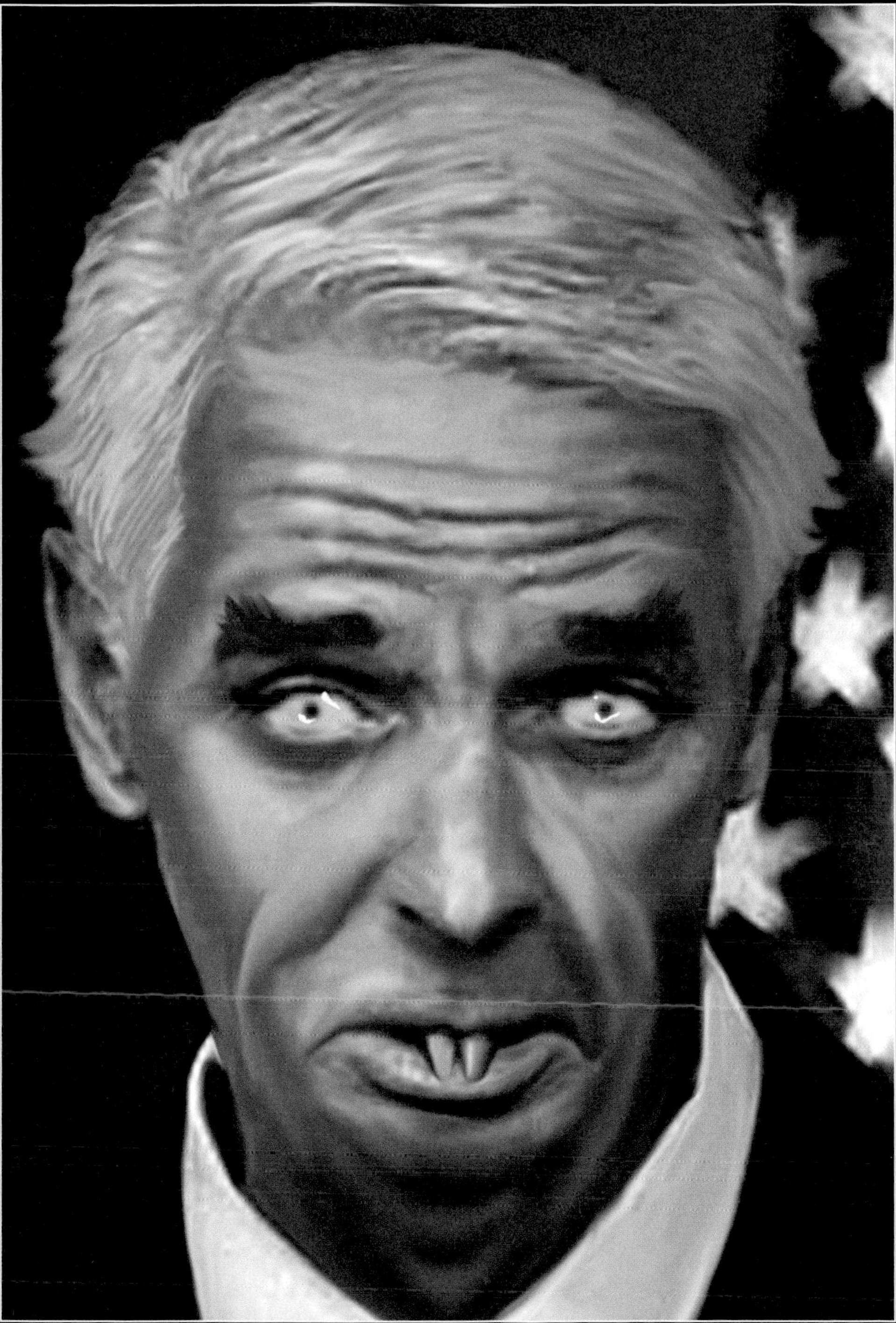

EMPTY-HEADED South Carolinian Jim DeMint is a towering leader in the United States Senate. The problem is, he has no followers. He's a strong voice for a coalition of Senators that includes Jim DeMint and, um... no one else, really. He's too right-wing lunatic fringe even for Senate conservatives. In the past, he's said things like how he wants to make health care reform "Obama's Waterloo" —by which he means a great defeat for the whole nation. Like Whitney Houston on a half bottle of Darvon, DeMint seems to have a reckless, nothing-to-lose attitude. He single-handedly torpedoed a nominee for a top security job because the candidate was supportive of unionized workers. Yes, it's worth putting America's safety at risk to keep working people down. Because it's so lonely for him in the Senate, he has sought love and respect in the arms of another. He has trolled Tea Party gatherings, shooting off his mouth. Teabaggers are so excited that a real-life United States Senator gives them the time of day, they've made him a folk hero. Like Napoleon. At Waterloo.

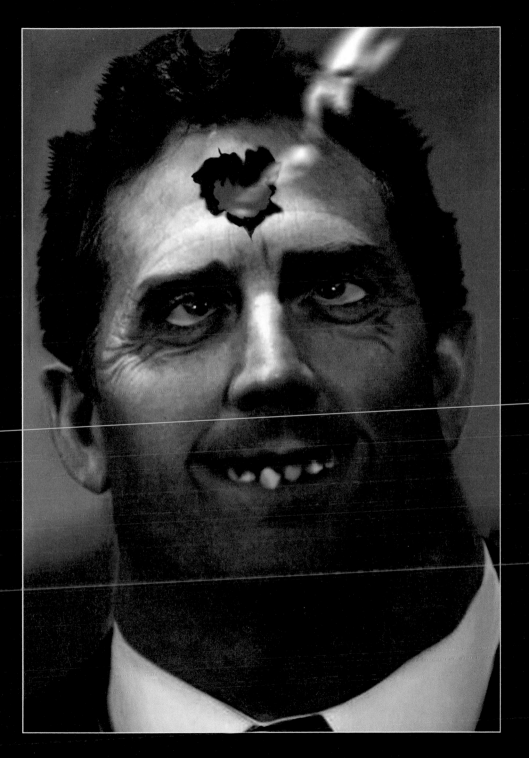

LOU DOBBS (aka "La Migra") built a rather nice career for himself by cozying up to Wall Street and taking speaking engagement fees from people he was reporting on as a "journalist" on a show called "Moneyline." Can you say "conflict of interest"? He then got his own show on CNN, filling up endless tedious hours of airtime whining about "illegal aliens" (although, as an aside, he never uses the phrase "legal aliens"). His claims fall into the usual mantra Repuglicans use against the people that scrub our toilets, pick our food and wash our dishes; they're stealing our jobs! But he's added a twist, because apparently he gets bored of listening to himself talk about the same things all the time. So this is what he came up with: "illegal aliens" are spreading leprosy. Yes, leprosy! Apparently only the undocumented immigrants are the problem because disease knows if your papers are in order. C'mon, Papillion, there's no evidence to support this outrageous claim, but you knew that, didn't you? Check his documents (let me zee das pay-perz!) because someone might want to deport him to keep him from spreading his verbal leprosy.

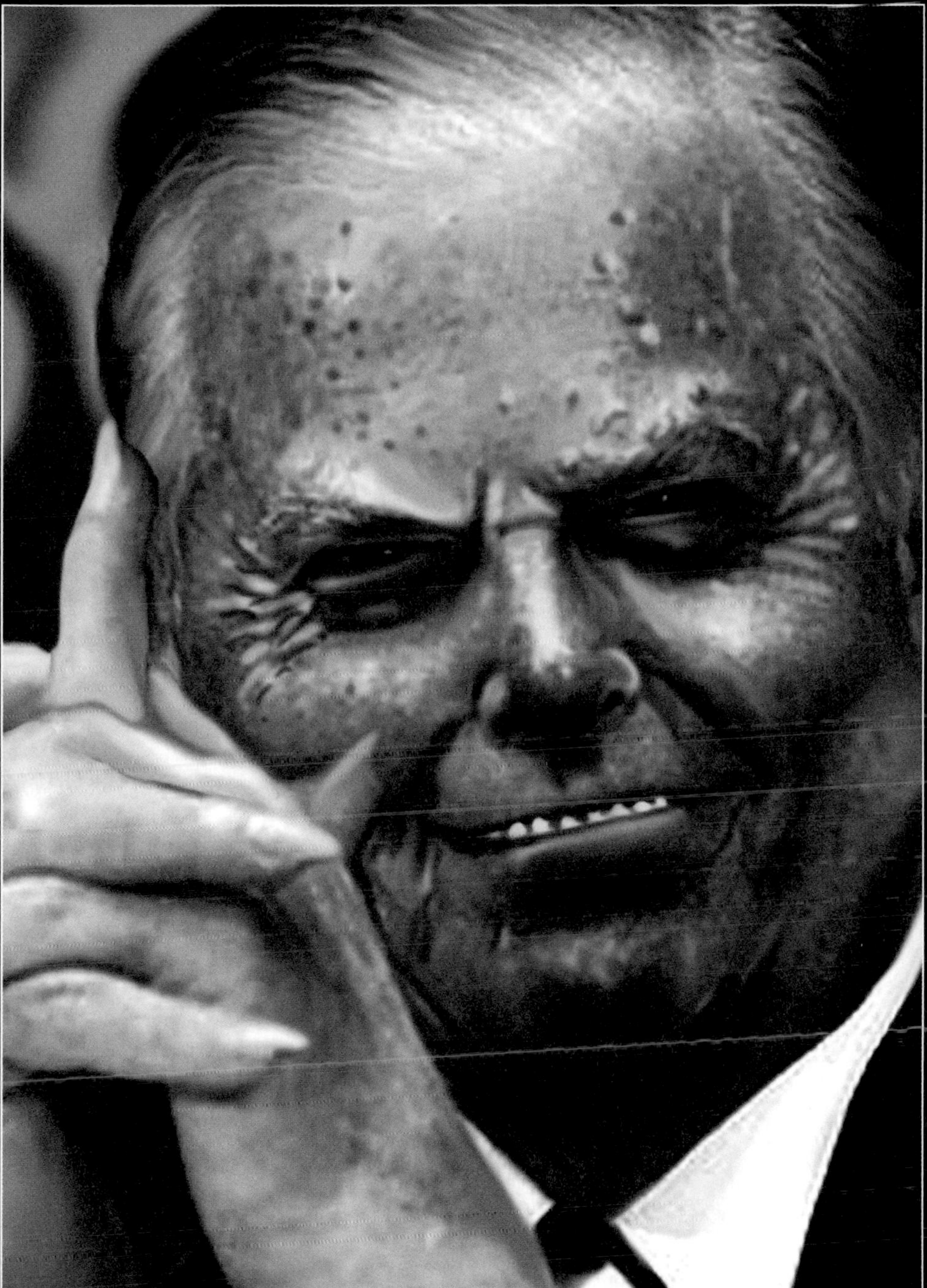

## THE TEN COMMANDMENTS OF JAMES DOBSON

I. Thou shalt hold onto thy beliefs, such as belief that any destruction of major American cities is due to the fact that God justifiably hates lesbians.

II. Thou shalt not watch SpongeBob SquarePants, because that might make thee gay.

III. Thou shalt equate same-sex marriage to marriage between men and donkeys.

IV. Thou shalt stuff thy true feelings way deep down inside where no one can see them.

V. Thou shalt say the President of the United States is going to ban the Boy Scouts.

VI. Thou shalt deny the existence of science, dinosaurs, global warming, stem cell research, and the roundness of the Earth.

VII. Thou shalt say creepy things like, "He can even take his son with him into the shower, where the boy cannot help but notice that Dad has a penis, just like his, only bigger."

VII. Thou shalt use a switch or paddle to beat thy children. A belt is best for the family dog.

IX. Thou shalt support display of Ten Commandments monuments carved from stone in front of all public buildings.

X. Thou shalt portray all who disagree with thee as Nazis

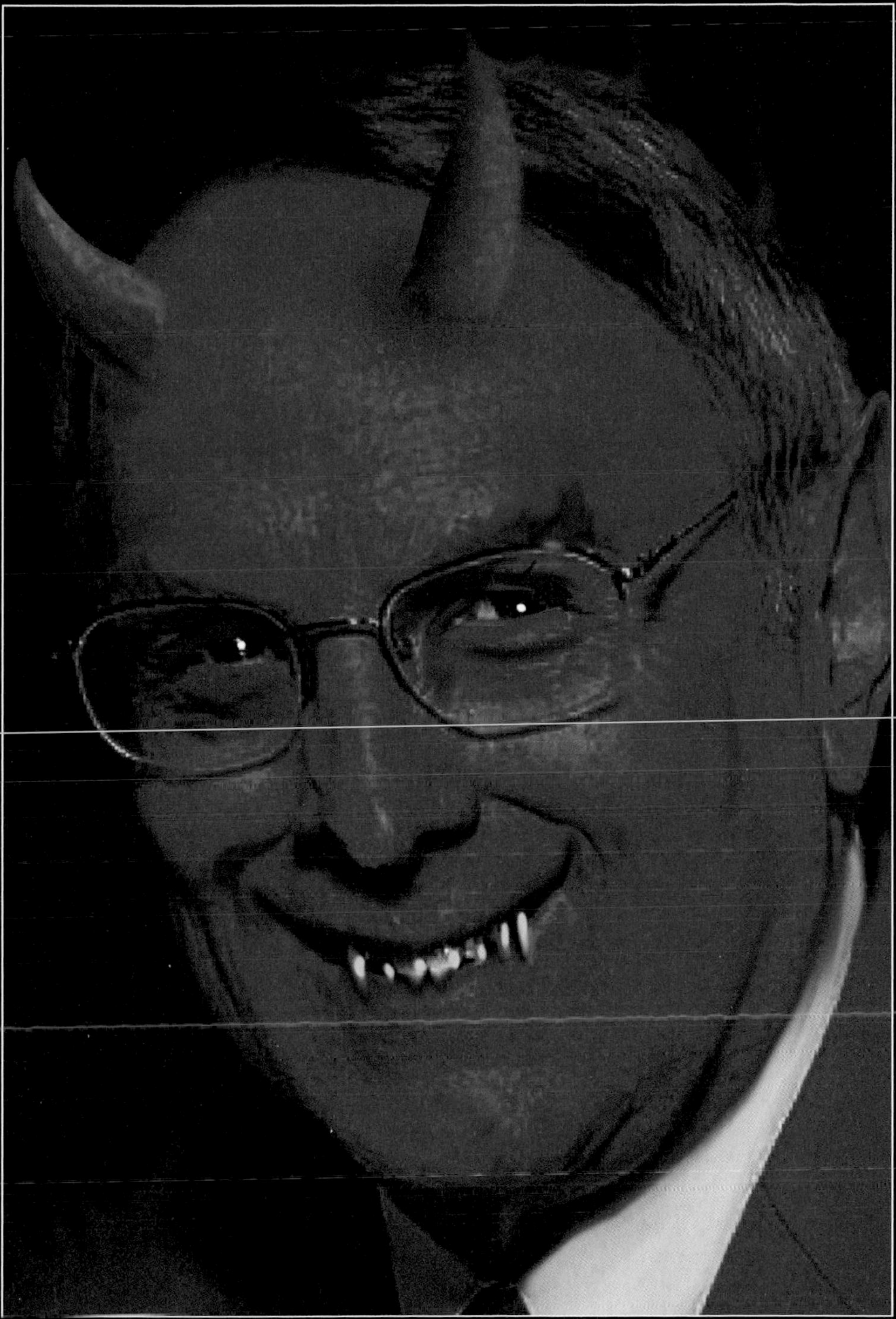

SURE, the Senator is a "family-values," born-again Christian, a member of a Pentecostal church and the Promise Keepers. And he cheats on his wife. And he pays hush money to people to keep quiet about it. Lots of money. And he lies about it. That's just not enough to cost you your job anymore. When people like John Edwards can run for president while hiding their love child, I guess America's scarcest resource is shame. Does it matter that Ensign called on Bill Clinton to resign over his affair? Or that he suggested Larry Craig resign over propositioning someone (despite the lack of an actual affair or hush money). But, really, it's not the senator's fault. He has campaigned for "traditional" heterosexual marriage and tried at every turn to thwart the rights of gays to marry because, clearly, those same-sex relationships are a threat to all "real" marriages like his. When a handful of states legalized gay marriage in the early 2000s, obviously that's when the senator's marriage unraveled, proving that those marriages did indeed threaten his own. If sensible people everywhere had simply continued to oppress same-sex couples, John Ensign's marriage could have been saved. It's a real shame.

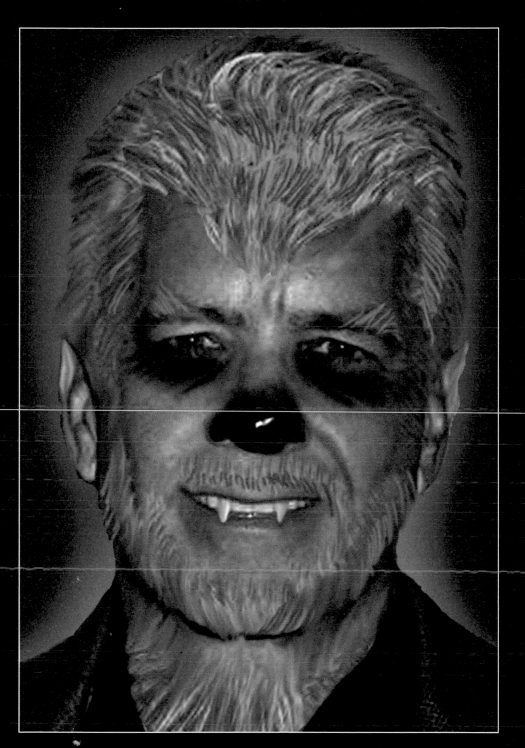

DEADBEAT DAD and serial adulterer. With all those achievements under his rather substantial belt, you'd think this college professor would be satisfied. However, he was desperate to add "Congressman" to his resume. And he did! On his third try. Upon taking office, he immediately divorced his wife (because, he said, "she isn't young enough or pretty enough to be a president's wife") while she lay in her hospital bed after cancer surgery. He would later cheat on wife #2 with the woman who would become wife #3 as he led the charge against President Clinton for his affair with Monica Lewinsky. Perhaps because his freakish alien fingers are two feet long, he just can't keep them out of trouble and away from tainted money. He was confronted with 84 ethics charges while he was Speaker of the House of Representatives. Yes, he was eventually cleared of most charges (he is a lawyer and he was in charge after all); he admitted he misled the Committee on Standards of Official Conduct. Eventually Gingrich stepped down after the GOP suffered massive losses during 1998's House elections.

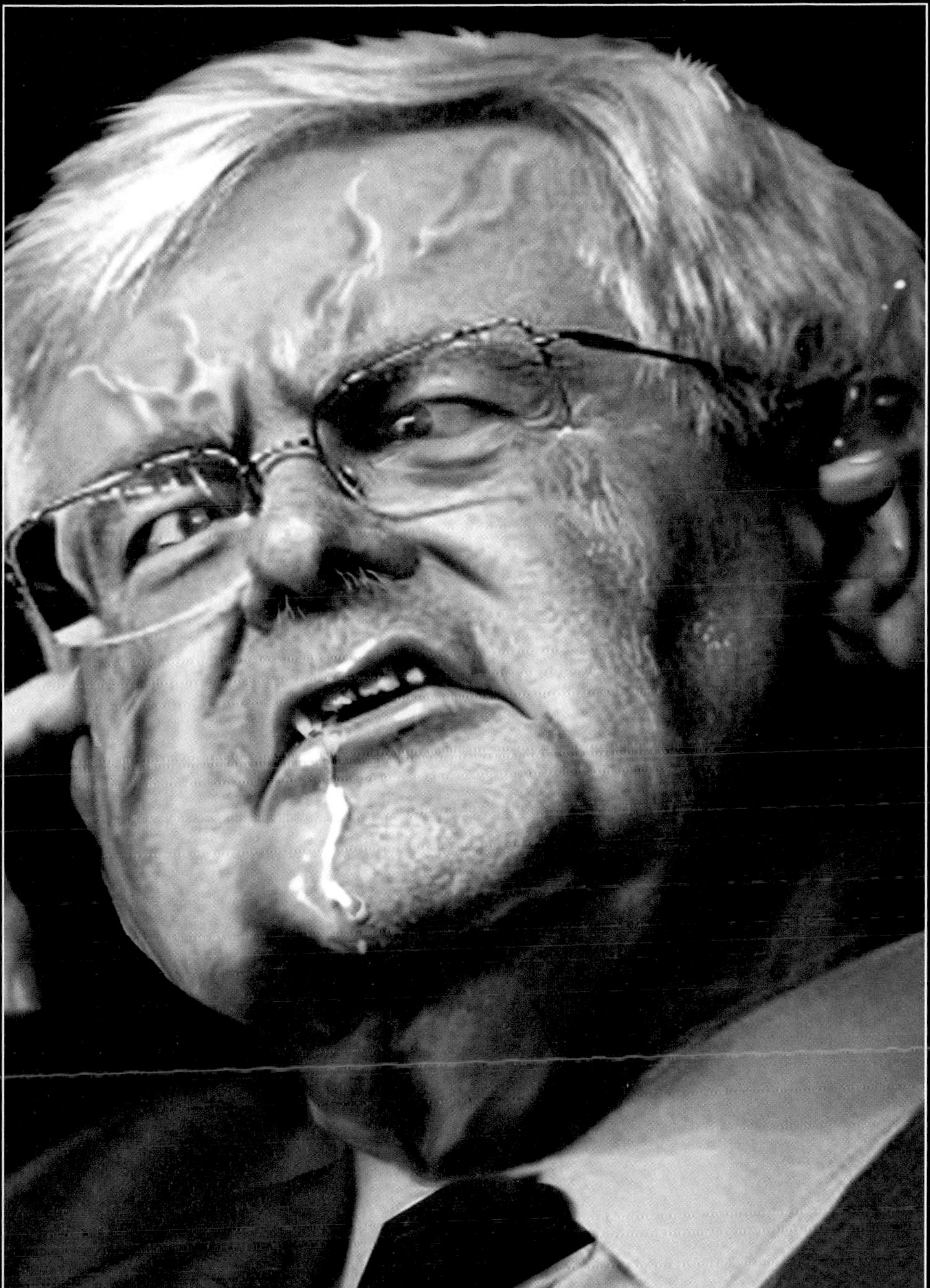

A PROFESSIONAL campaign dropout, Rudy Giuliani has quit electoral races more often than he's cheated on his wives. The man tried to parlay the random coincidence of being the mayor of New York during the 9/11 terrorists attacks into being elected leader of the Free World. Being that he couldn't get more than a handful of voters to support his career ambitions, he tries to fill that empty space inside with paid speaking engagements, where he presumably puts on a hard hat and yells into a megaphone about how he wants to kill Muslims, while tuxedo-clad, Chardonnay-sipping audiences cheer. He wants us to say, "You had me at 9/11." But the magic is gone. Yes, he still haunts us, but not in the way his lovelorn mistresses go ga-ga over him. He lives on in our minds as the creepy pre-"Mayor of America," comb-over, dressed-in-drag Rudy. He now hangs around banquet halls signing autographs like an ex-high-school football captain loitering in his old school's parking lot, wearing his letterman jacket and sporting a "Hey, remember me?" look on his face. Beware the Ghouliani.

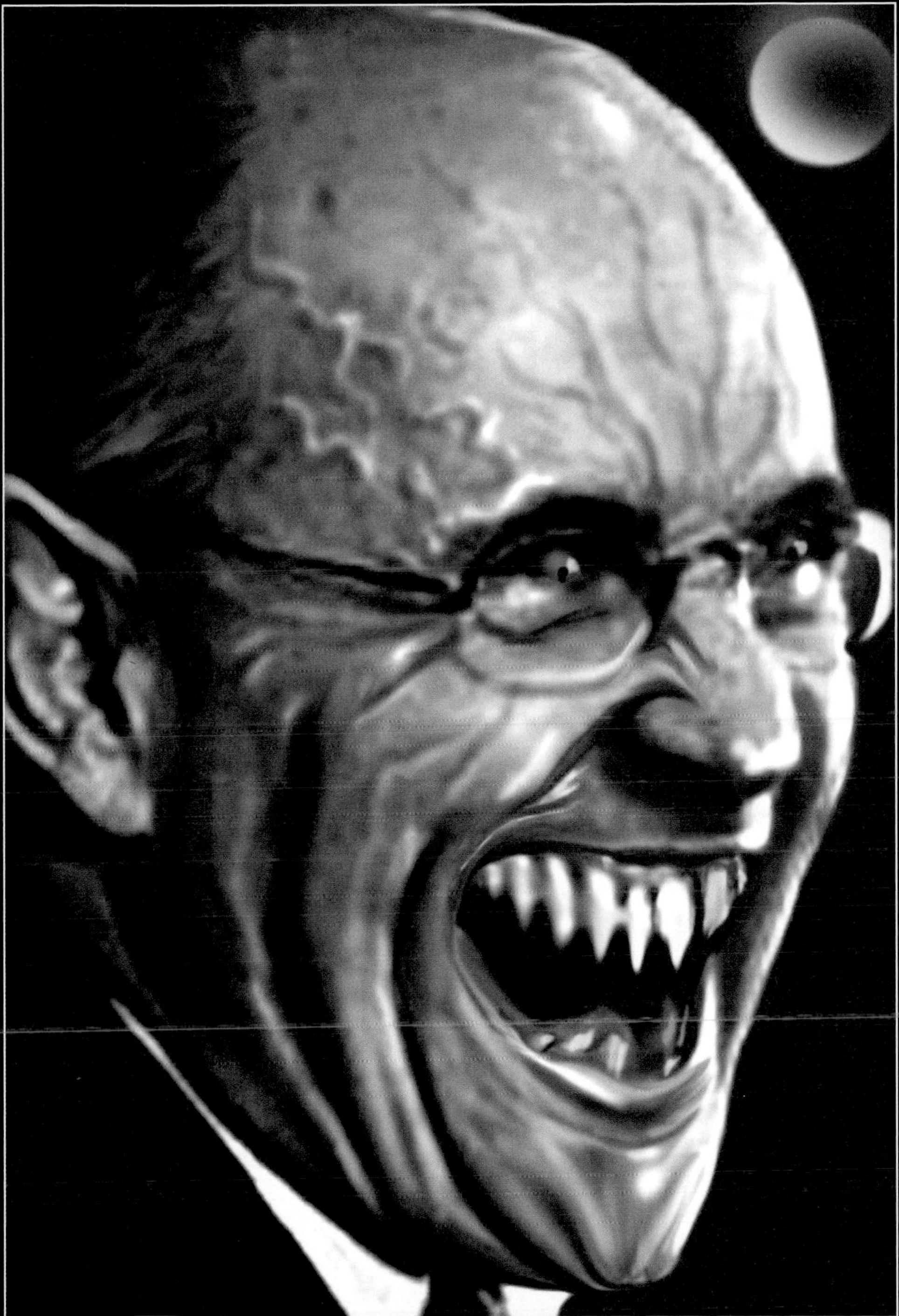

JONAH IS THE OFFSPRING of Lucianne Goldberg, an accomplished opportunist, who honed her people skills trolling D.C. cocktail parties for dirt as a spy for Richard Nixon. She knows a good opportunity when it lands in her lap. She encouraged Linda Tripp to tape conversations with Monica Lewinsky. We have her to thank for Lewinsky keeping the blue dress. As the media besieged Lucianne's apartment during the Lewinsky scandal, her son Jonah rallied to Mommy's defense in a piece in *The New Yorker*. It launched his career as a professional right-wing mouthpiece. He now divides his time equally between denying the science of global warming and penning diatribes like his tedious tome *Liberal Fascism*, in which—your dead Grandpa who fought the Fascists in World War II will be sad to hear—Franklin Delano Roosevelt is outed as a Fascist. Although he appears frequently on television, it is little known that he is never seen below the waist because he sports a set of eight slithering tentacles. This is because whenever he spews forth, he hasn't got a leg to stand on.

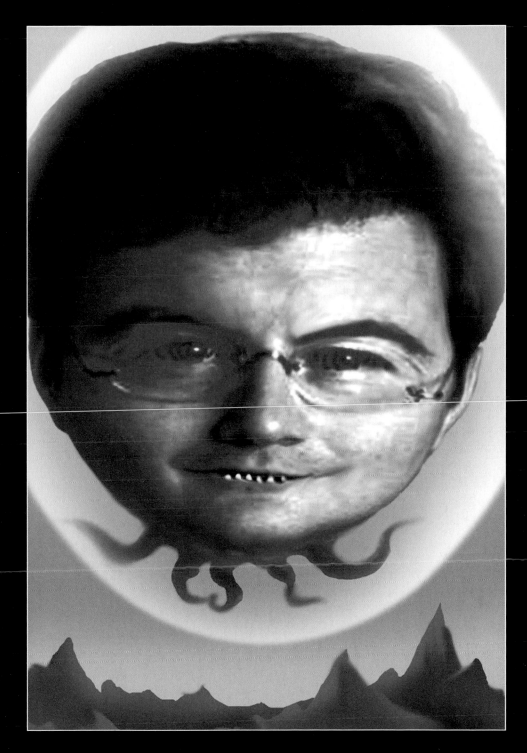

WHO'S THAT pandering sycophantic creature standing in John McCain's shadow with his tongue caressing the Senator's backside? Why, it's little Lindsey Graham! Or, as he's referred to by McCain affectionately, "Little Jerk." Despite his nickname, he's not too fond of sticking up for the "little guy." Lindsey is making it his life's work to deny people health care. He is against health care reform because he has decided that the process of creating the legislation back in 2009 was "seedy, Chicago-style politics." Now, Chicago-style pizza sounds pretty tasty, but we're not so sure about the seeds or what it has to do with health care. But if denying health care to the poor doesn't do away with them, he has a Plan B. Lindsey was first to bloviate against government contracts for ACORN, an organization that does horrible things like helping homeless people find housing and register poor people to vote. And nothing outrages Repuglicans more than those voting poor people with housing. I guess if, like government contractor Blackwater, they had mowed down 14 unarmed women and children in the streets of Baghdad, they'd still be getting their taxpayer-funded checks today. Now that's seedy.

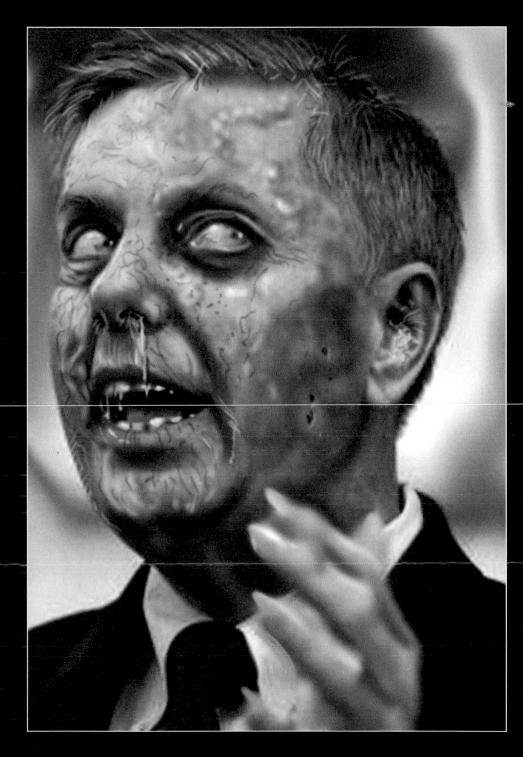

PRIVATIZE DEATH SQUADS! Iowa Senator Charles Grass-ley, an open-mouthed fish of a presence in the Senate since about 1912, is a fan of good ol' American private enterprise. He wants private insurance companies to decide whether you live or die, not some bureaucrat. Well, yes, some bureaucrat, but one getting paid by a private company with no public account-ability. This is why Grassley tried to scare the public by saying the government would "pull the plug on grandma." He hates government, which is kinda confusing since government pays for his food and house. He abhors people who are helped by government too, which is why he described Hurricane Katrina victims as "on rooftops complaining for helicopters to rescue them, and you see it on television too much." No Chuck, we see you on television too much. Despite the fact he hates govern-ment, the Senator had the nerve to say that President Obama doesn't have the experience to know how government works. The next time Grassley tries to tell Obama the way things are, the President needs to do what Lucy Ricardo should have said to Ricky all along: "No Ricky, YOU can't be in the show."

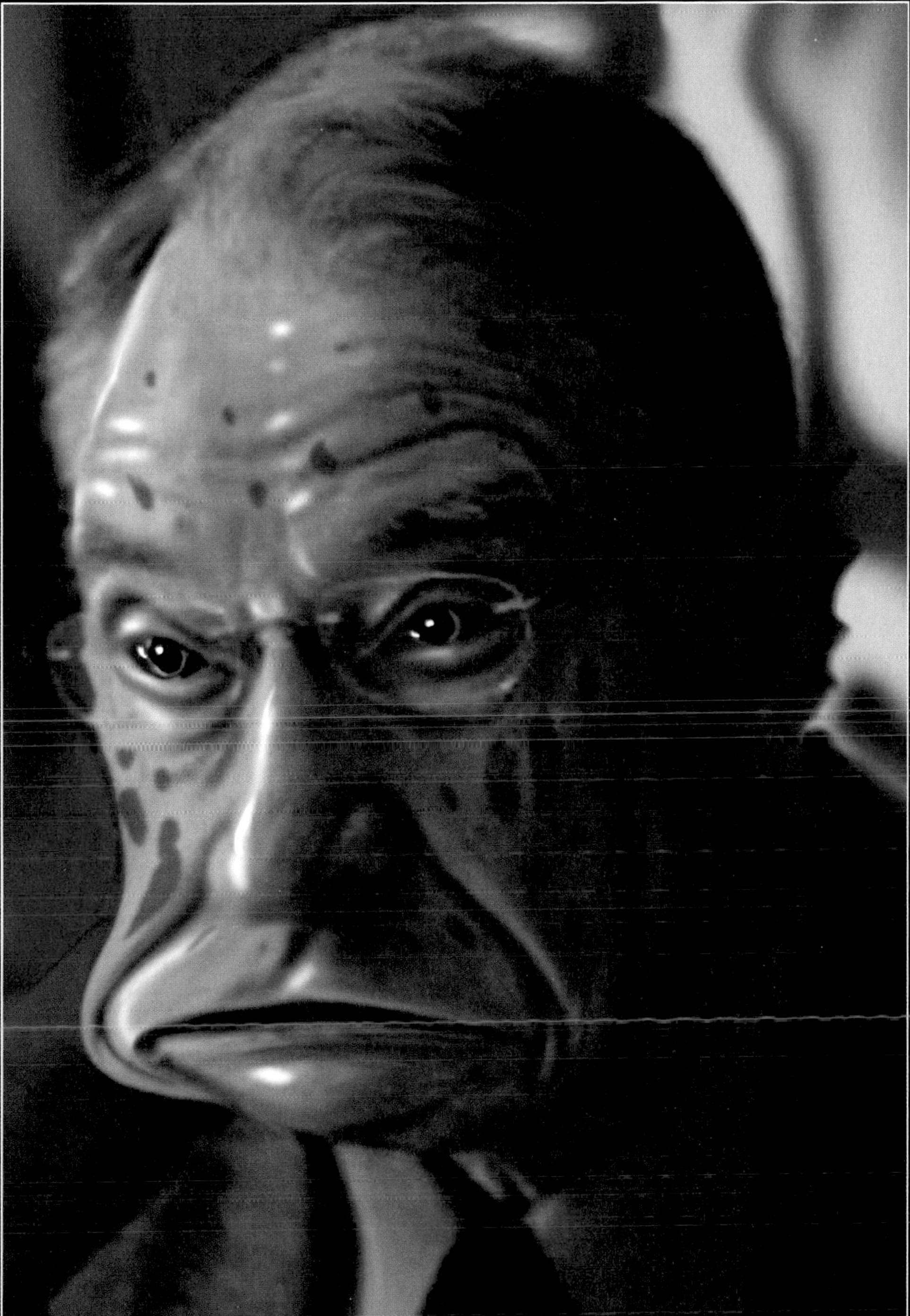

COLLEGE DROPOUT Sean Hannity got his start in college radio, where he specialized in gay-bashing (Sean to lesbian caller: "I feel sorry for your child") and buying newspaper ads telling the world how awesome he was. He worked his way up the radio ladder spewing hate speech ("Ted Kennedy won't be happy until we have mass slaughter in Iraq.") and later made a full-time career being a George W. Bush apologist. He's been known to pal around with terrorists like neo-Nazi Hal Turner, who posted bomb-making tips on his website for those who wanted to kill "savage negroes." Naturally, Fox News gave him a show. They hired an inept "liberal" co-host, whose name escapes everyone (Alan Colmes... I looked it up) who Sean could steamroll. The concept was to make Sean look brilliant, but the studio wasn't big enough for Colmes, Hannity and Hannity's ego, so Colmes was out — though few noticed his disappearance. The renamed show, "The Sean Vanity, er... Hannity Show," was a smash. What did Sean do with all this success? He created a website called "Hannidate" where gays (and straights) can hook up to experience Conservative-on-Conservative-Sean-Mannity action. Oh, yes he did.

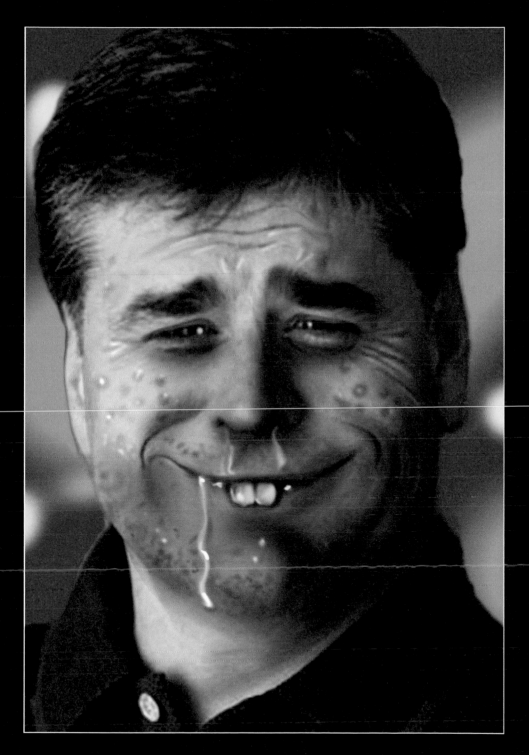

IT WAS REPORTED on November 12, 2001 that a media consortium of major U.S. news organizations determined that a review of all statewide votes using any of four different standards for counting all the votes (ranging from any marks or dimples to fully punched ballots) would have resulted in Gore winning the statewide election and thus the presidency. Katherine Harris ain't as dumb as that face painted on her face looks. She knew this was the likely outcome, and it was her job as a loyal Repuglican commissar to make sure the truth didn't get out. The plan, as everyone knows, was a success. Court papers were filed, thugs were flown in to disrupt proceedings, misinformation was fed to the media, and Harris, above all else, made sure all the votes were never counted. George W. Bush would be the person signing the paperwork, but Florida's Secretary of State, the powerhouse in the St. John knit, put Dick Cheney in charge of the Free World. Let's just put it this way, this woman has given more people jobs than George W. Bush ever did.

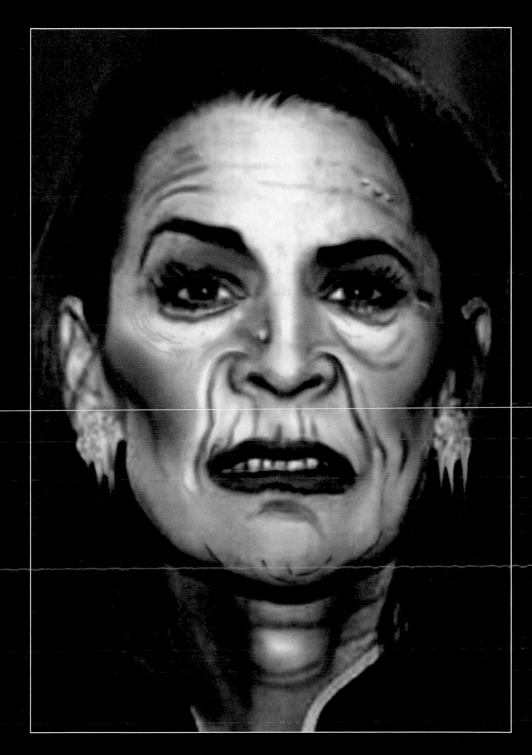

ORRIN HATCH WRITES MUSIC. U2's Bono suggested to the conservative Senator from Utah that he write under a pen name. When Hatch asked him why, he said, "Well, um, because you're you." Taking an assumed identity might be a great strategy for the Senator when attributing some of his quotations. Like when he said the Constitution is "ambiguous" about polygamy. And this gem: "Nobody denies that [Saddam Hussein] was supporting al-Qaeda…Well, I shouldn't say nobody. Nobody with brains." And let's add this classic to the Hit Parade: Terrorists "are going to throw everything they can between now and the election to try and elect Kerry." To be fair, the last one has some validity. No one was thrilled to see George W. Bush serve a second term. It's the part about anybody being super-excited about Kerry that's hard to buy. Hatch has written many bills opposing gay marriage, stem cell research, reproductive rights, and civil disobedience. While they are all extremely funny, none can rival the hilarity of his song, "Eight Days of Hanukkah." He sings too, and when he does, he chirps like he's part of a chorus of locusts about to descend upon us like the plague.

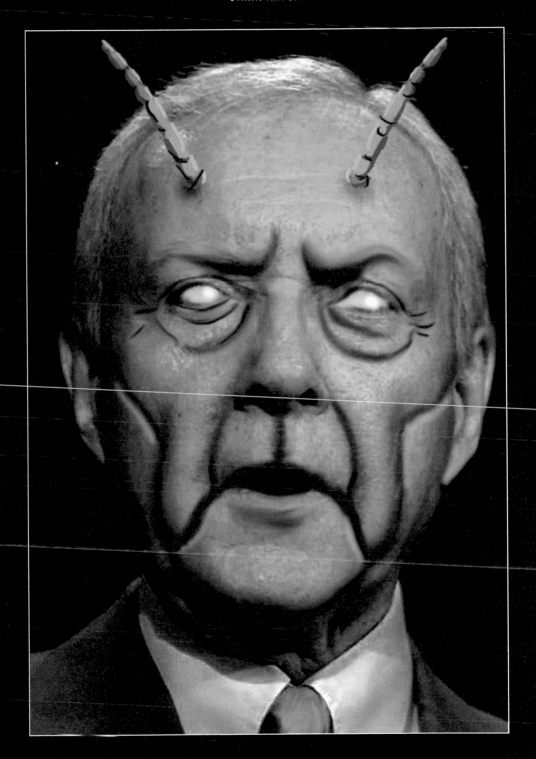

COME AND LISTEN to a story 'bout a man named Huck,
A poor evangelist, barely kept his family truck,
Had a vision one day while shootin' at some grouse...
And he saw himself livin' in a big White House!
President that is, Commander-in-Chief, head honcho.

First thing you know ol' Huck's a millionaire,
Donors said " Hey, Huck, get the heck away from there!"
Said "Washington is the place you wanna be,"
So he stumped out on the trail that would lead to D.C.
The Beltway, that is. Cocktail parties, lobbyists.

Well he hasn't made it yet but he's on the Fox News.
A place where he can chew the fat and let ya know his views.
You're all invited back again to this locality
And don't forget in twenty-twelve to vote for Huckabeeeee.

Capitol Hillbilly that is. Pray a spell. Turn your brain off.
Y'all come back now, y'hear?

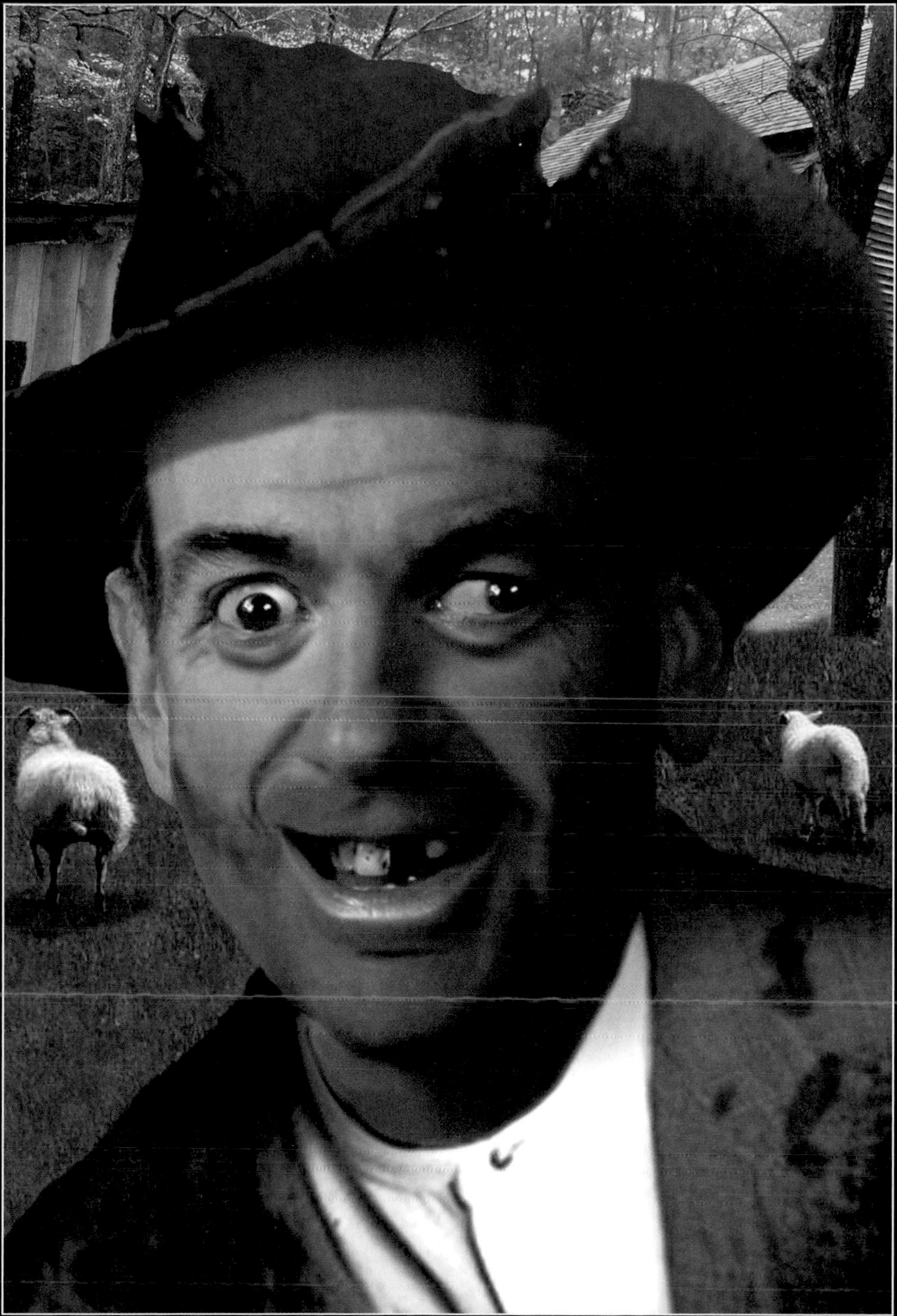

IT'S A GOOD THING Oklahoma Senator Inhofe doesn't believe in science, because then he'd be faced with the reality that genetics have caused him to pass on his ignorance to his offspring. In February of 2010, the Inhofe family built an igloo, put a sign on it that read "Honk if you ♡ global warming" and posted it on Facebook. Idiotic, yes. Immature, certainly. But just think how blissful this whole family must be in their world without science tests. Takes some pressure off those Inhofe kids. Inhofe has compared scientific theories about global warming to Hitler's perpetuation of Nazi Propaganda. You really have to wonder how that makes any sense to anyone. Apparently Inhofe hates history as much as he hates science. He seems to have a generalized fear of knowledge. The stupid, it burns! But seems he hates the gays even a little bit more. He actually said, with, undoubtedly, a straight face, on the Senate floor: "I'm really proud to say that in the recorded history of our family, we've never had a divorce or any kind of homosexual relationship." Many congratulations to the Senator and his entire family, though it's possible there's some inbreeding somewhere.

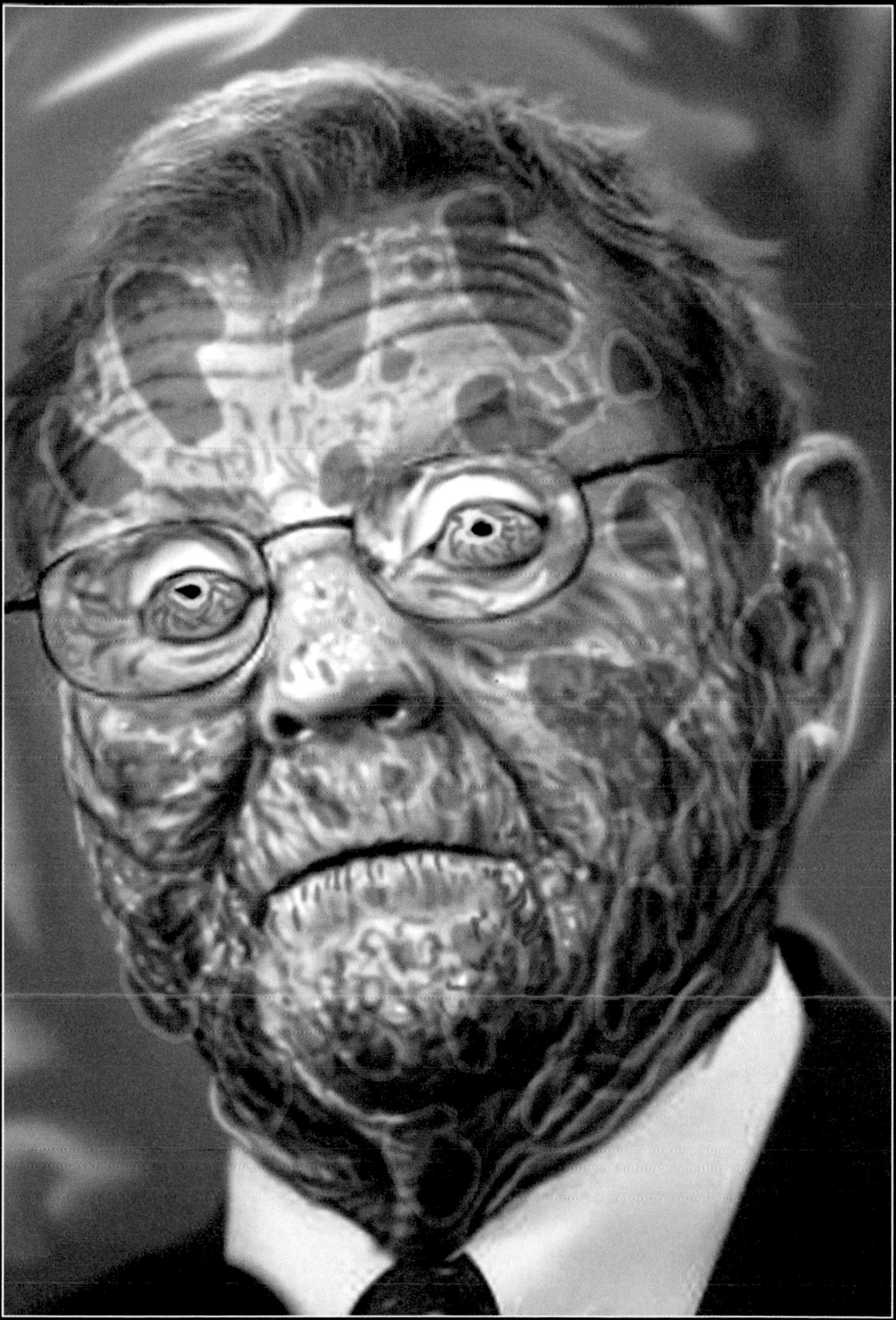

LITTLE PIYUSH JINDAL changed his name to "Bobby" because he wasn't super-crazy about being named "Piyush" while growing up in Louisiana. So he named himself after a character on the Brady Bunch. No word yet on whether his wife, Supriya, has any intention of renaming herself "Marcia, Marcia, Marcia." He also switched from being Hindu to Catholic. It's unclear what else he hates about himself, but very near the top of the list must be his performance on February 24, 2009, when he gave the official GOP response to a speech by President Obama. Let's just say his speech couldn't have been received worse had he been selling swastikas in the Catskills. He is trying to bring many changes to Louisiana as its governor: the introduction of intelligent design into its schools, chemical castration of its prisoners, and oil drilling to its shores. He's also decried the use of government stimulus money publicly while taking the money privately. He has brought about slightly fewer improvements to the state than did Hurricane Katrina (which he mentioned in that February 2009 speech, by the way, because it was an awesome idea for Repuglicans to remind people of that moment in time).

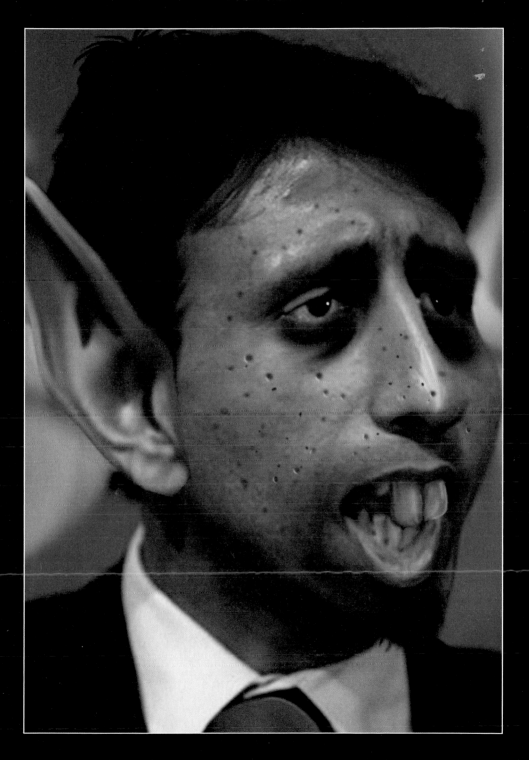

THE REPUGLICANS' GIFT is the ability to whip the country into a frenzy against a common enemy (most recently, Islamic militant jihadist terrorists, in other words, anyone who wears a turban) in order to control the hearts and minds of America. Repuglican Congressman Steve King of Iowa knows this game well. He said that if Obama is "elected president, then al-Qaida, the radical Islamists and their supporters, will be dancing in the streets in greater numbers than they did on September 11th." I missed that dance party. Maybe that's what was actually on TV when I thought I was watching the MTV Inaugural Ball. Of course, King's credibility isn't great. He's the guy who said Joseph McCarthy was a "hero for America." King is not shy about holding unpopular opinions. When Congress went on record passing a resolution 399-1 acknowledging our nation's capitol was built by slave labor, guess who was the single vote against it. That's right, our friend Steve King. Okay, so we know what he's against, but what is he for? Well, cockfighting. Yes, he wants to legalize cockfighting.

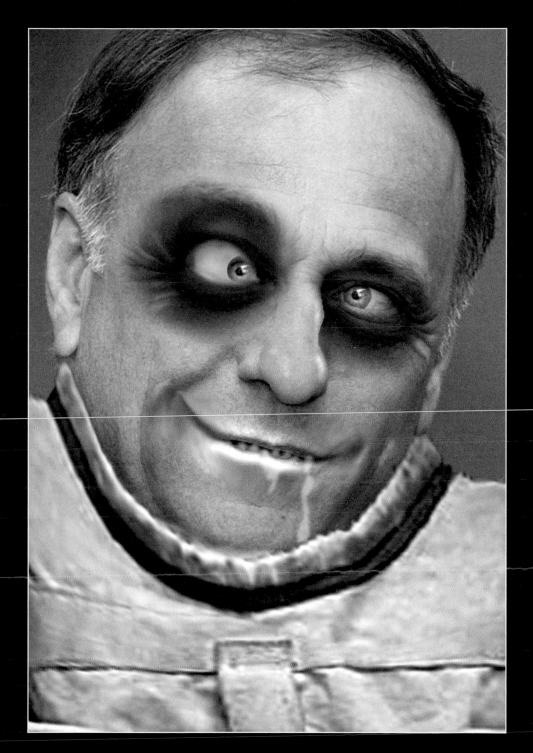

NOT TO BE CONFUSED with actor Billy Crystal, although the confusion is understandable because they are both hilarious. One of them knows nothing about politics and the other is a beloved actor. *The Weekly Standard* editor and columnist William Kristol is the son of Irving, who is the godfather of the neo-con movement; you know, those people who want to make the Middle East a better place by blowing it off the face of the map. Kristol Jr. said, "I want to hear less about helping the Iraqi people and more about winning this war." Uh, I thought they were supposed to be the same thing. Guess I missed a meeting. If you ever wonder where President Bush Jr. got his brilliant foreign policy ideas, many of them came from this guy. He certainly had the resume for it, being the former chief of staff for Vice President Dan Quayle. Kristol was known as "Quayle's Brain," which is a great gig because you can do it with one lobe tied behind your back. Explains why Kristol's crystal ball is a bit fuzzy. He's made endless predictions about the glorious, triumphant United States victory in the Iraq war... all wrong.

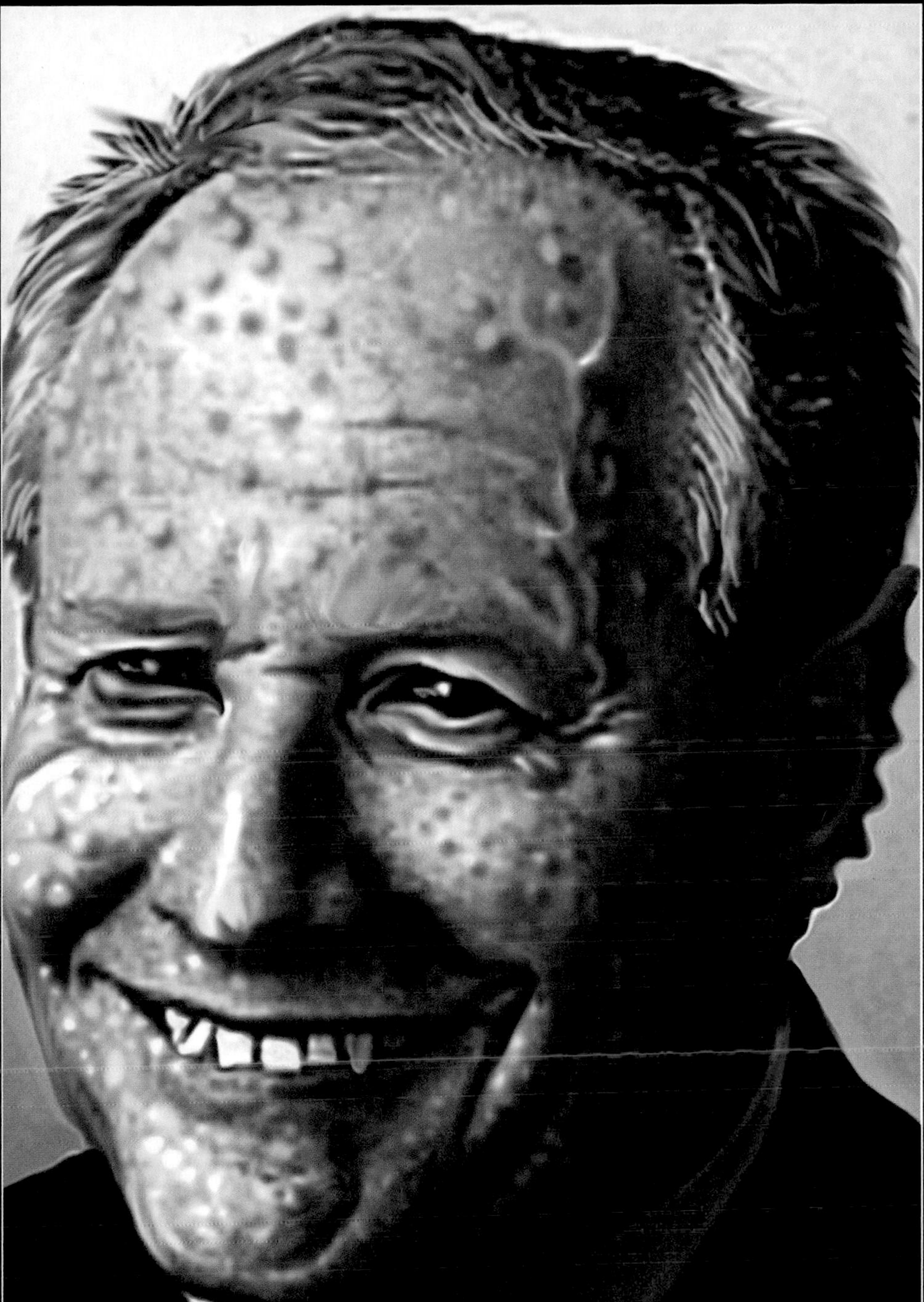

THE SECRETARY GENERAL of the United Nations condemned it as "offensively anti-Islamic." The President of the European Union said its only effect is "inflaming hatred." In contrast, Senator Jon Kyl of Arizona not only celebrated it, he organized a screening of it in the Capitol: a 17-minute film called *Fitna*, in which Quran verses are juxtaposed with terrorist attacks. Nothing incendiary about that. It's not so bad that Kyl would show a movie that deliberately encourages discord among faiths at government expense, but this movie got a 5.2 rating on IMDB.com. A 5.2? Seriously? C'mon, *G.I. Joe: Rise of the Cobra* got a 5.8. Our tax dollars are paying for our representatives to spend their paid time watching a movie that can't earn a score from audiences as high as *I Now Pronounce You Chuck and Larry*. Kyl may not like Middle Eastern governments but he doesn't seem too keen on America's either, holding up the nominations of six important Treasury appointments in the Obama administration because of the White House's delay in implementing a pet anti-gambling initiative of his. Way to get the economy moving, Senator. Maybe his time is better spent at the movies.

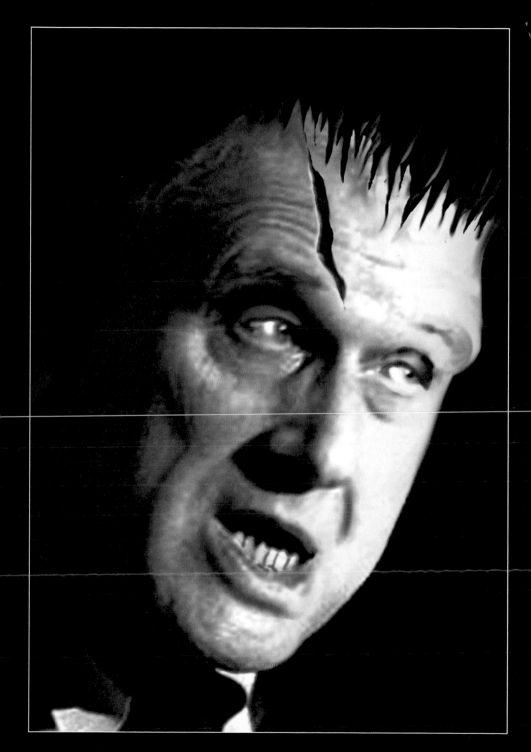

ing cries against the government. Here's one of his gems: if a government official tries to disarm someone, he advises the public to fight back by going "for the head shot; they're going to be wearing bulletproof vests... Kill the sons of bitches." That's good, practical stuff. What is the source of this wisdom, insight and courage? Liddy himself says listening to Hitler's speeches as a child "made me feel a strength inside I had never known before." He is the Bronze Bullet Repuglicans need to inspire them to action.

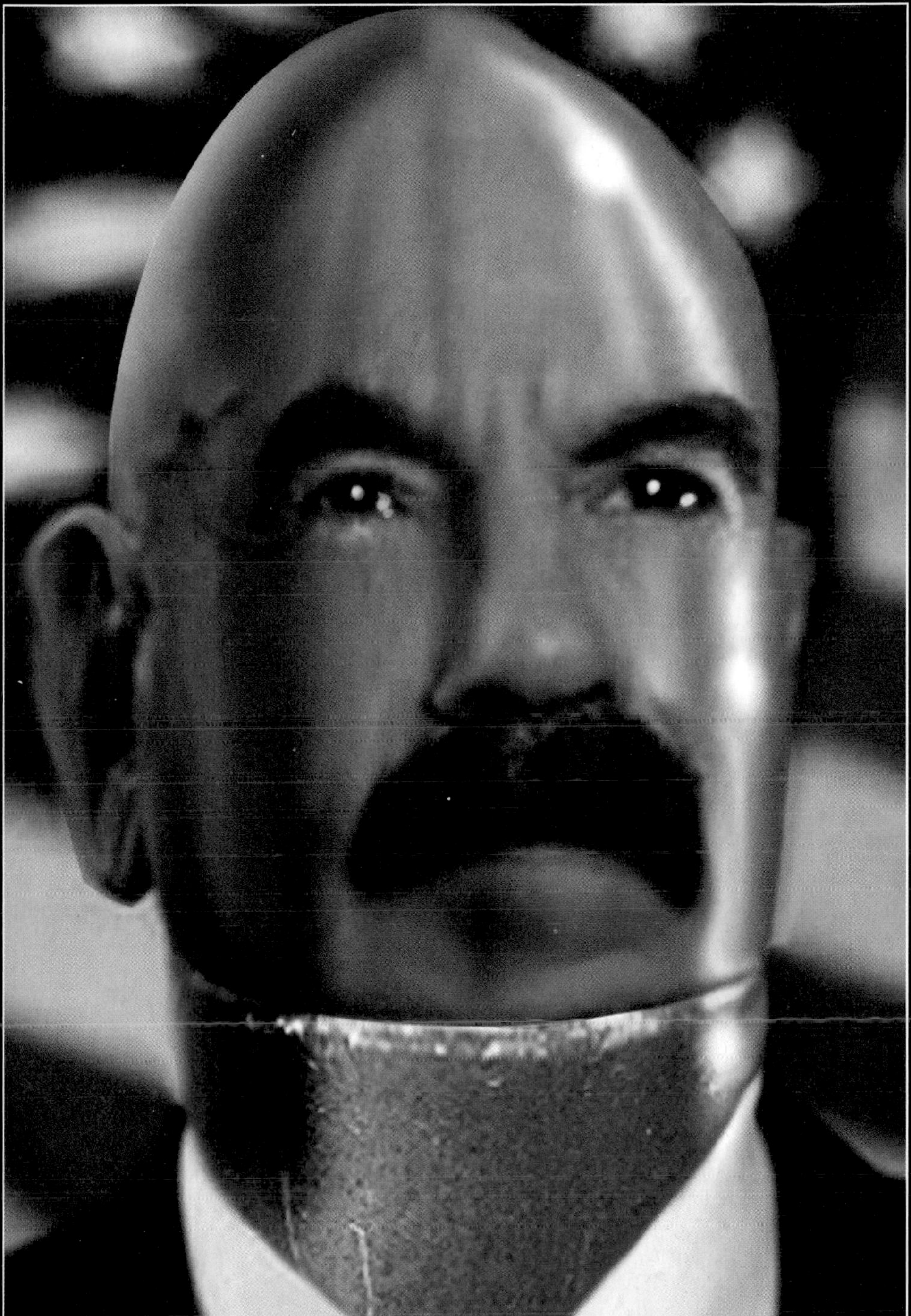

I DO NOT LIKE that man named Joe.
I never know which way he'll go.
He was a friend but then no more.
Seems he's very much a whore.
Is he right or is he left?
Of true allegiance he's bereft.
A man of lousy etiquette
A Grinch who stole Connecticut.
I do not like him here or there.
I do not like him anywhere.
You can have that wrinkly goat
Who sold his soul and then his vote.
I liked him more pre-nine one one.
Now the man is just no fun.
He's gripped with fear down to his bowels
Arab hate fills up his jowls.
All Joe-mentum is long gone,
And his dull speeches make me yawn.
I'm sorry to see him go.
I miss the sweet old Joe.
Before he hung with those Repuglican dicks,
He was a Jew who worked hard for us 24/6.

JOE LIEBERMAN

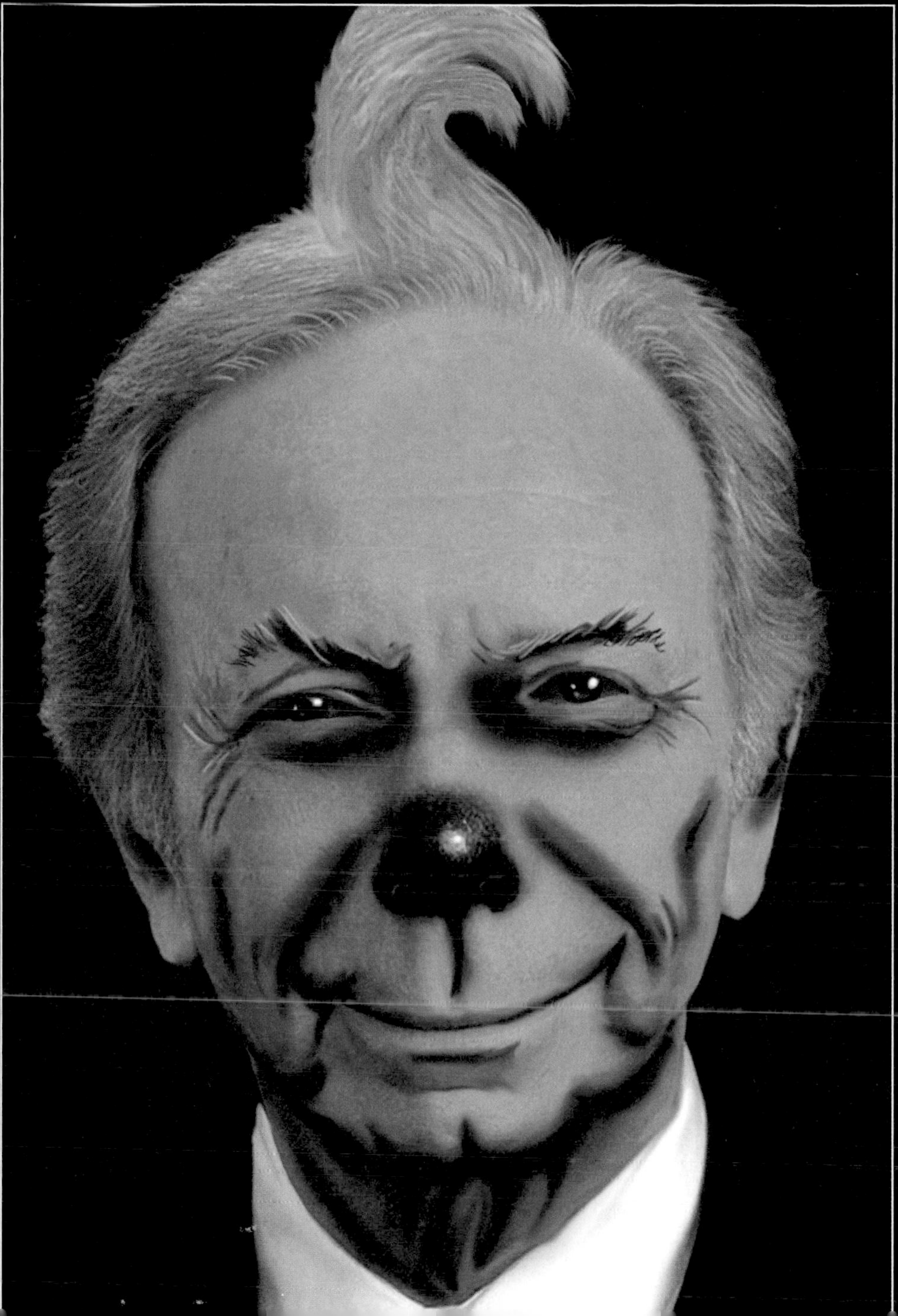

A HIGH SCHOOL DROPOUT, drug addict, and big tub o' goo, the bloviating windbag has undoubtedly done okay for himself thanks to an army of hypnotized zombies that hang on his every word when they're not busy gunning down abortion doctors or putting Jesus fish stickers on the bumpers of their SUVs. Limbaugh has been brought to earth to harvest human souls, which he does via a daily syndicated radio show. He's now one of the highest paid junkies on the planet, not counting Cindy McCain. What does he get paid for? Making fun of Michael J. Fox's Parkinson's, saying things like "Have you ever noticed how all composite pictures of wanted criminals resemble Jesse Jackson?", and arguing against helping aid the people of Haiti after the earthquake that killed tens of thousands and left hundreds of thousands homeless. I'm sure for him it's soul-enriching, life-affirming work. For most of the rest of us, just to listen is more painful than a face full of needles.

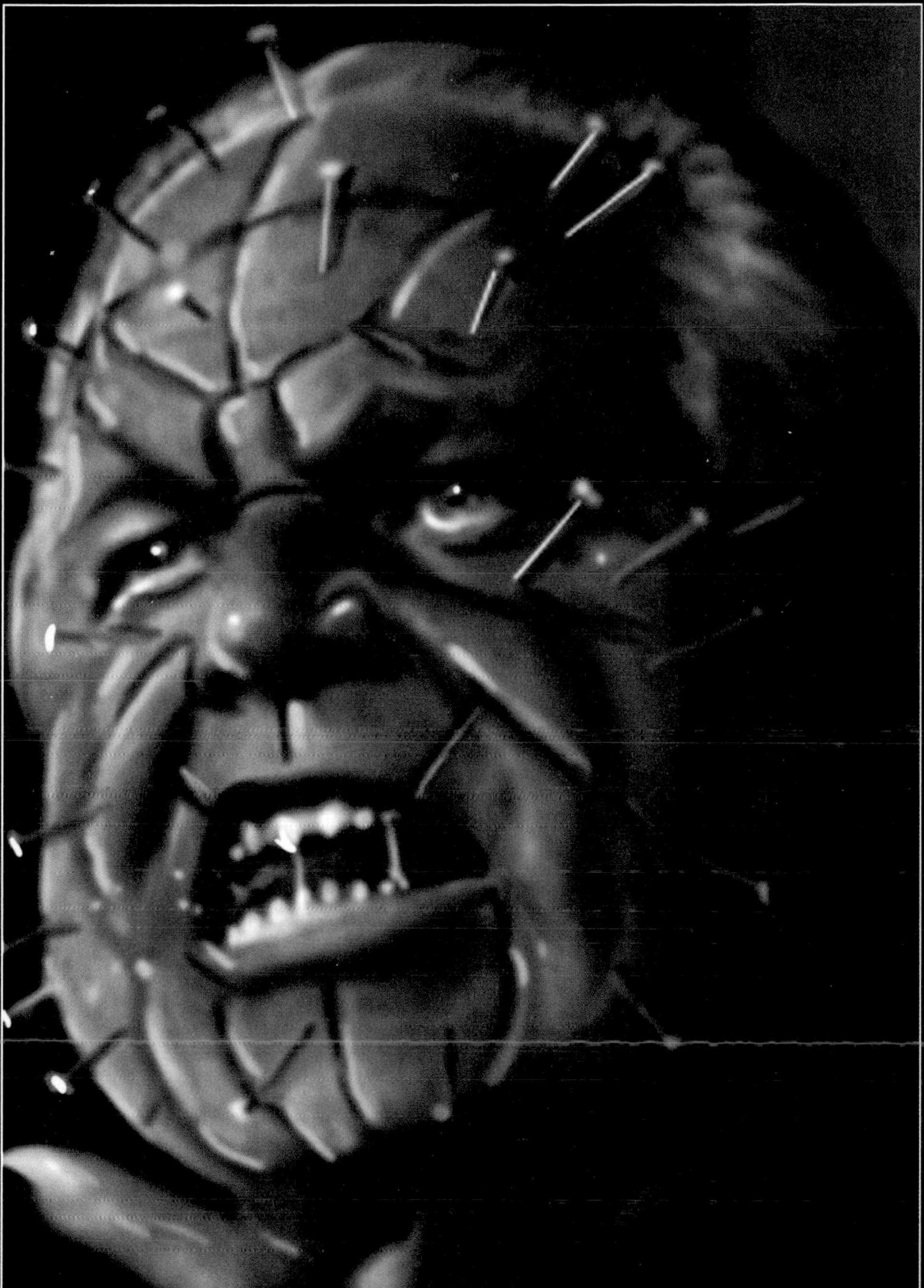

MICHELLE MALKIN is the author of a book defending the internment of Japanese-Americans during World War II and advocating the same treatment for Arab and Muslim-American citizens today. Michelle Malkin's co-worker at Fox News, Geraldo Rivera, had this to say about her: "Michelle Malkin is the most vile, hateful commentator I've ever met in my life. She actually believes that neighbors should start snitching out neighbors, and we should be deporting people." He felt the need to add, "It's good she's in D.C. and I'm in New York. I'd spit on her if I saw her." Guess they won't be carpooling to the studio together. As a seasoned attention-whore, her only objection to being called the "Asian Ann Coulter" is that she insists she's not Asian, though both her parents are foreign-born Filipino nationals. It is thought that she rummaged through Ann Coulter's trash and ingested enough of Ann's bodily fluids to cause a zombie-like transformation. Michelle's family later called in an exorcist to try to cast the demons from her, but she continued to spew hateful speech and coarse language, frightening children at holiday gatherings. Oh, and she's Asian.

MICHELLE MALKIN

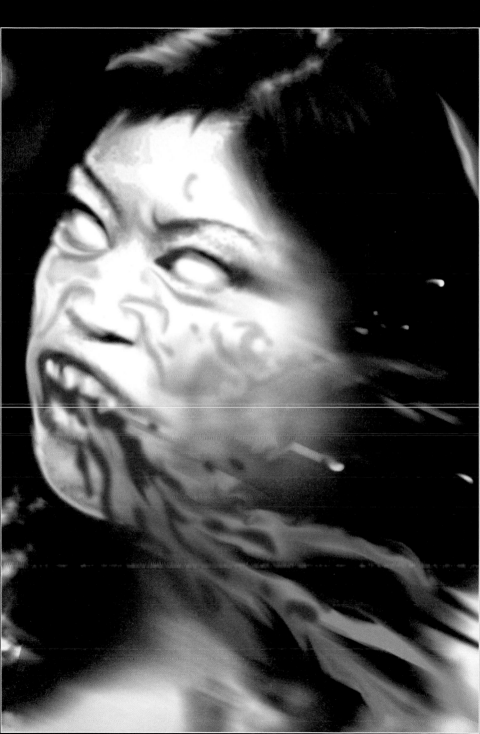

## THE JOHN MCCAIN QUIZ

### A maverick is:

A) A crazy character played by Mel Gibson

B) A crazy character played by Tom Cruise

C) A crazy character played by John McCain

### That bulge on McCain's cheek is:

A) Where he keeps Cindy's stash

B) Mini-Me

C) Why you should always wear sunscreen

### McCain picked Sarah Palin as his running mate after:

A) Carrot Top turned him down

B) Talking to Nancy Reagan's astrologist

C) Palin's witch doctor cast a spell on him

### Conservatives don't like John McCain because he:

A) Doesn't talk enough about Jesus

B) Thinks immigrants are people

C) Thinks

### John McCain is so old that he remembers when:

A) It was just the Keating 4

B) Bob Dole had his original hair color

C) He was a Republican

### "Straight Talk" means:

A) Tell people exactly what they want to hear and tell them it's "straight talk"

B) Campaign consultants earned their money

C) John McCain is working to turn around Lindsay Graham's sexuality

### John McCain lost the presidential election of 2008 because:

A) He couldn't get the stink of George Bush off him

B) Not enough Joe the Plumbers voted

C) He's John McCain

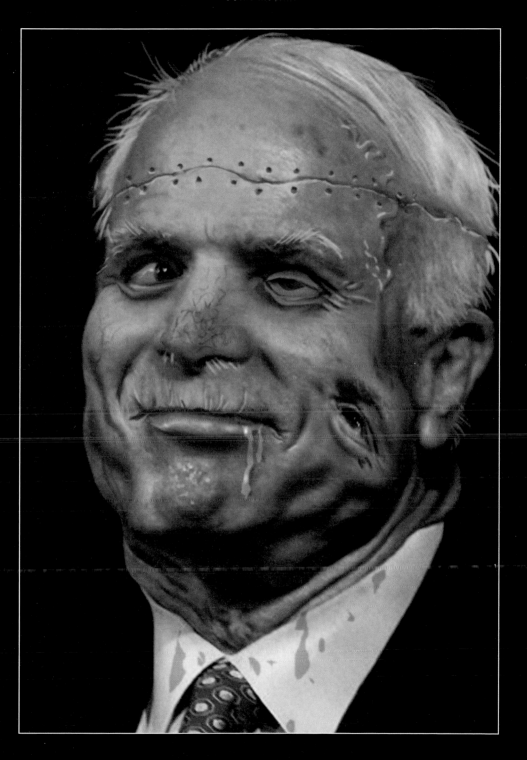

THIS MAY BE SOMETHING you've experienced in your life: knowing a pathological liar. For some reason, she says atrocious things about you and your friends. It causes stress, disruption and worry. You want her to get help. Mostly, you just want her to go away so you can talk with your friends about that crazy person who almost ruined everything. America has such a person in our collective life. Betsy McCaughey. She lies about health care. She wouldn't think twice about ripping your heart out with her bare fist if you wanted to provide health care for the poor. She's not an important person, but she knows important people, so she gets to be in newspapers and on TV to talk about how every effort at health care reform—Clinton's, Obama's—is the single most dangerous thing ever created by mankind and will kill your grandma. She lies so much she doesn't even know she's lying. She's the O.J. Simpson of the health care debate and, like O.J., she gets away with it. She's the one you can thank for cooking up the crazy notion of "death panels." Perhaps her words could avail themselves of one.

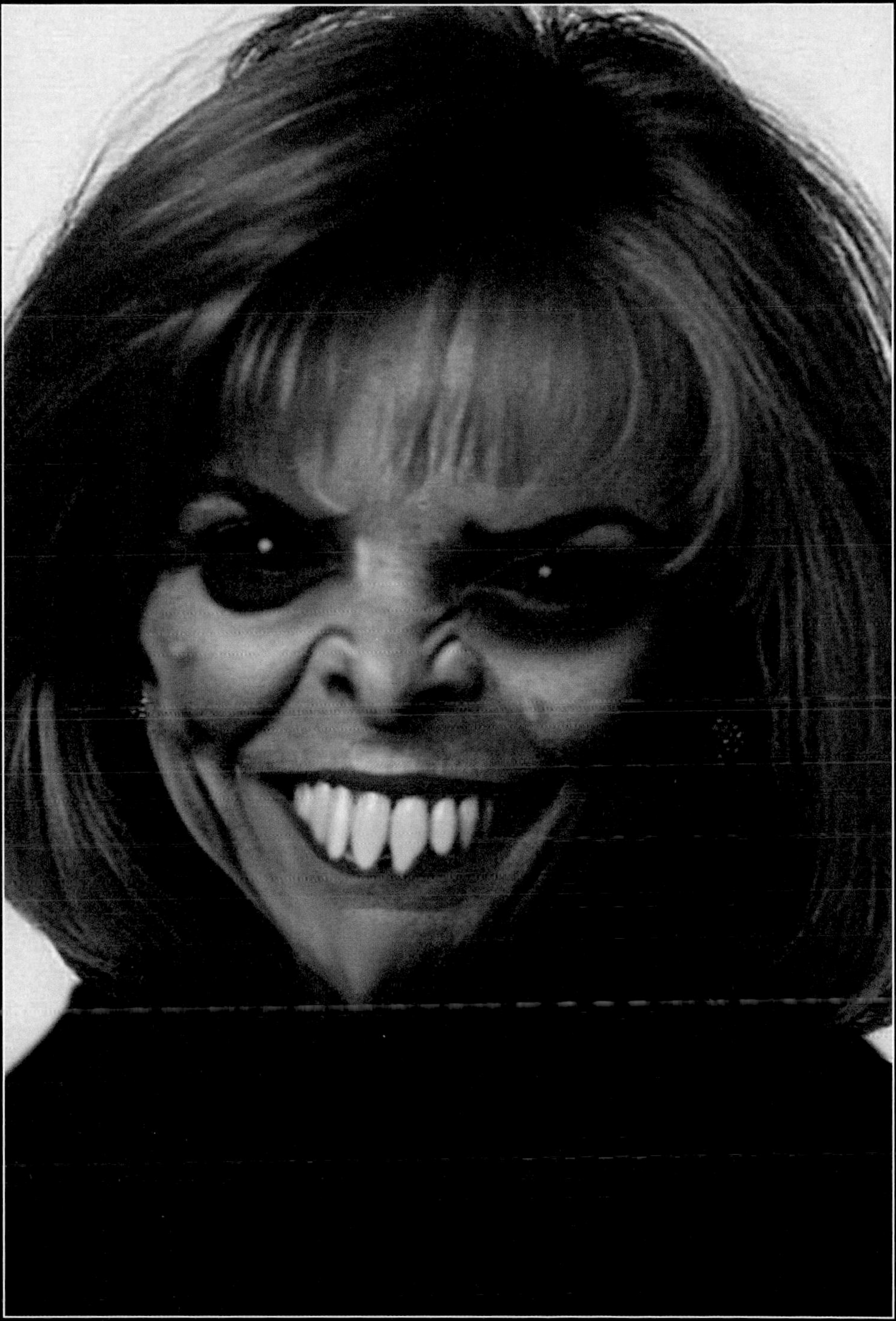

IN 1996 HE DEMANDED Clinton officials testify under oath. Cut to 2007, the other party's in power. McConnell says it's not appropriate for Karl Rove, Harriet Miers, and other Bush officials to testify. In light of this tendency, one understands his first campaign slogan: "Switch to Mitch." Mitch likes to switch positions. Not political stances. He's a died-in-the-wool partisan whose face is melting from all the energy generated by his constant fillibustin'. It's the rationales used to justify his actions, which are, let's say, "flexible." He's both for and against Medicare and has stated both views simultaneously on his website. As Minority Leader in the Senate he's switched the meaning of "filibuster" from a seldom-used legislative procedure to how the Repuglican Senate goes about its daily business. Under Switch McConnell, since 2008 his party has attempted to filibuster an unprecedented 100 percent of the Democrats' major initiatives. In 1993 he switched wives and is now married to Elaine Chao, President Bush's Secretary of Labor. He had to switch. It's what he does. Someone save her from Switch before he switches again!

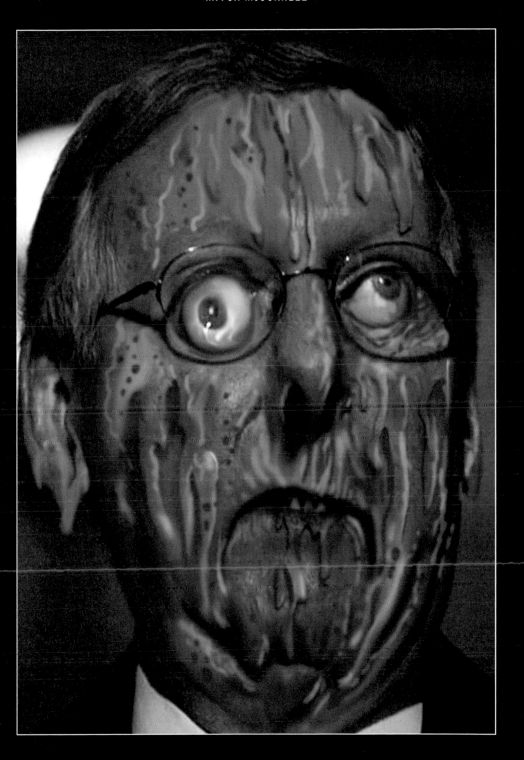

NOBODY LIKES HOMEWORK. Who wants to learn all that science and history? Well, good news for future generations; soon, school will be completely devoid of any facts at all. Hooray! Who do we thank for this? Why, it's Mr. Don McLeroy! He's no fan of book learnin', he ain't. He favors Creationism. That's where science goes something like this: God makes everything up. Congratulations, you're now an expert in "Creation Science." McLeroy is also the former Chairman of the Texas School Board, the biggest buyers of textbooks in the entire United States (flat-broke California has said they're not buying new books until 2014). So when Texas shops for books for 4.7 million kids, authors write whatever sells. If McLeroy had his way, textbooks would deny the separation of church and state, declare as fact that the Earth is thousands of years old as opposed to 4.5 billion, emphasize America is a "Christian nation," wouldn't mention Senator Ted Kennedy, and express McLeroy's worldview, typified by his question, "What good does it do to put a Chinese story in an English book?" So if you want to help your kid with his homework, better throw back a big, steaming cup o' stupid.

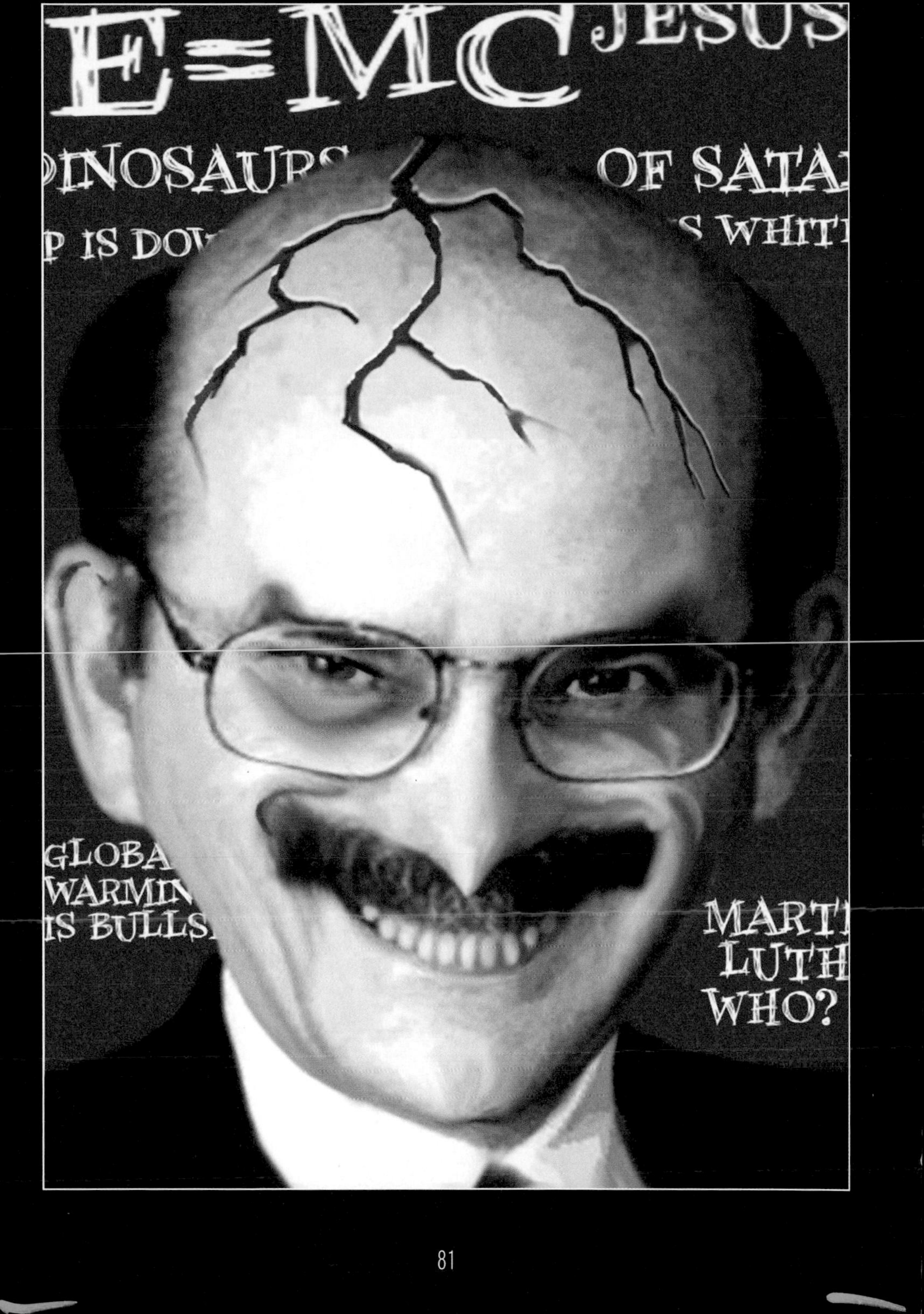
E=MC
JESUS
INOSAUR
OF SATA
P IS DOW
S WHIT
GLOBA
WARMIN
IS BULLS
MART
LUTH
WHO?

YOUNG COMEDIAN Dennis Miller steps up to a microphone to talk about the middle-aged Dennis Miller:

Hey, babe, this libertarian cat twists so far to the right that he could land a gig in Cirque de Soliel. The notion that he'll advocate an enlightened position is about as likely as J. D. Salinger showing up at your slumber party. He said he wouldn't make jokes about George Bush because he doesn't make jokes about his friends. Who is this guy, Hayley Mills? C'mon, Pollyanna, ease up on the schmaltz. He's become about as funny as a ruptured spleen. Dr. Kervorkian gets more laughs. To him, the war in Iraq is no more than a good start. He's so pro-war he won't even buy unleaded gas for his car. The bullets, babies… they're lead! Like Charles Foster Kane, he sits in his central California mansion taking inventory of his possessions. You can imagine him uttering his Rosebud, "Sinbad!"

It's rumored this man still wakes up in the morning as Dennis, but when the moon is full, he transforms into the right-wing ideologue even he can't stand. Quell our pain, Dennis babe, drive a stake through it.

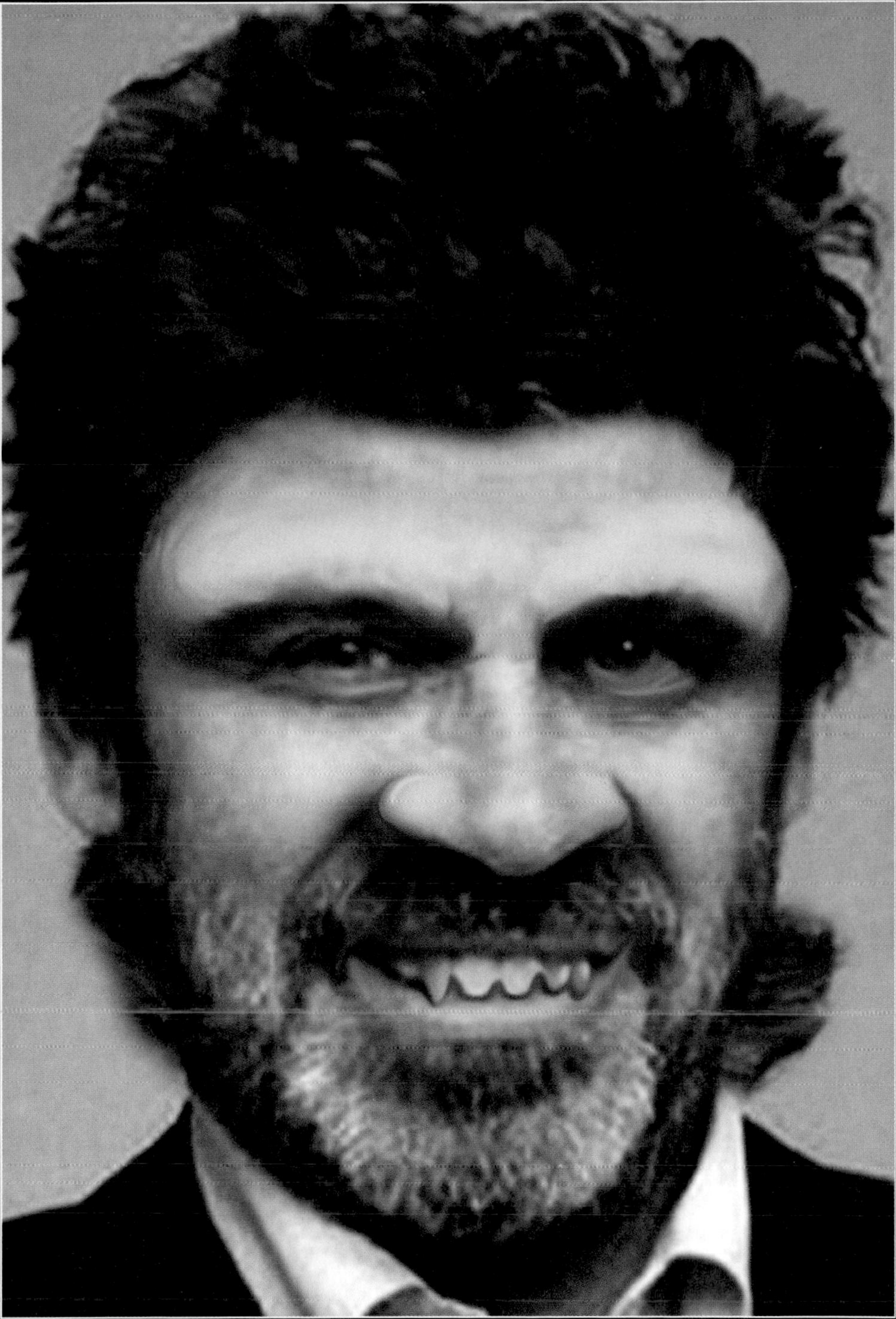

MURDOCH OWNS FOX NEWS, which calls itself a news network, even though it does things like Photoshopping people in unflattering ways if they say something critical of the channel, or putting a title over Michelle Obama, labeling her "Obama's Baby Mama" (Murdoch knows a thing or two about babies, having had a couple in his 70's... and having married three). Murdoch installed George W. Bush's cousin to oversee Fox's Election Night 2000 coverage and after spending much of the evening on the phone with his Bush cousins, "George the candidate and Jeb the Florida campaign chairman," John Ellis switched Fox's Florida call from the Gore to the Bush column. This cemented the false impression that Gore lost and that Democrats tried to steal a victory in court. But that's what all-powerful mad geniuses do—they make sure things turn out their way. And, according to one of Rupert Murdoch's own writers, Matt Labash, here is how right-wing media works: "We've created this cottage industry in which it pays to be un-objective... It's a great way to have your cake and eat it too. Criticize other people for not being objective. Be as subjective as you want. It's a great little racket."

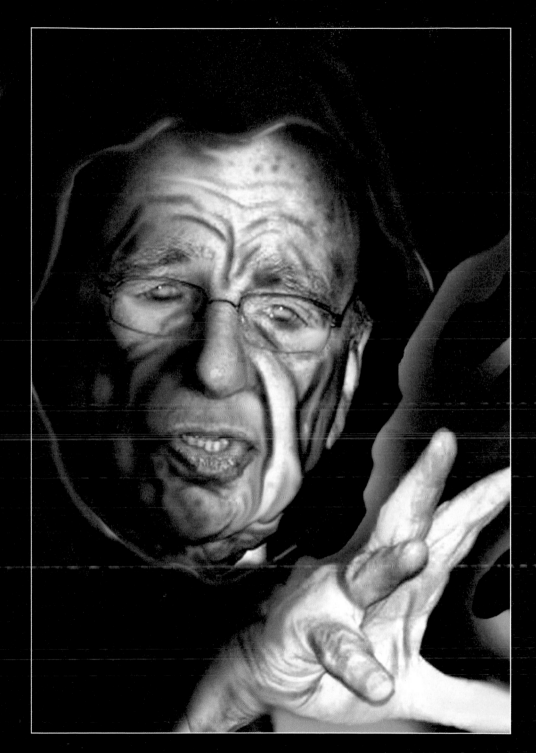

SOME FACTS ABOUT CHUCK NORRIS:

- Chuck Norris doesn't believe in helping the poor. He gives them roundhouse kicks.
- Chuck Norris has no use for the war on terror. He is the war on terror.
- Chuck Norris opposes health care reform. If anyone gets sick, he'll kill them.
- Chuck Norris should be on the Supreme Court because then we wouldn't have to have trials. He'll just stare down the facts.
- Chuck Norris could knock out the deficit with one hand tied behind his back.
- Chuck Norris doesn't mind global warming. He's cool enough for the whole planet.
- Chuck Norris thinks everyone should have a gun. Or a cuddly protective beard.
- Chuck Norris believes in giving people rights, as long as they're followed by lefts and upper-cuts.
- Chuck Norris doesn't believe in science unless, one day, it discovers why he's so awesome.
- Chuck Norris thinks God is on America's side and everyone else can suck it.

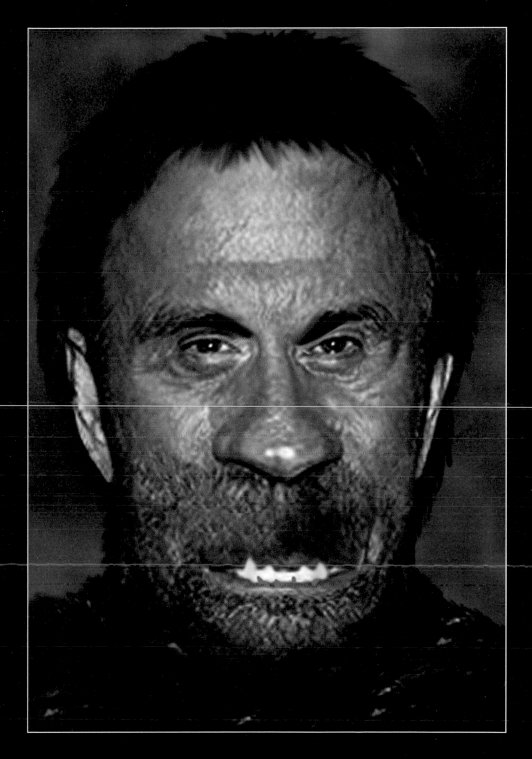

RIGHT-WING hot-air-machine radio host Laura Ingram wrote a book called *Shut Up and Sing* about how she doesn't enjoy entertainers exercising their right to have opinions. Perhaps she should have given her pal—flag-waving, gun-nut and lover of the wang dang and sweet poontang—Ted Nugent a copy. This would have prevented this super-patriot from saying regrettable things like "Obama, he's a piece of shit. I told him to suck on my machine gun. Hey Hillary. You might want to ride one of these into the sunset, you worthless bitch." But he has more on his mind than threatening the President and Secretary of State. The Nuge has a coherent, well-thought-out policy on Iraq that takes into account the fragile state of the Middle East and the role of civilians in Baghdad. Well, it's really more criticism than policy. The Motor City Madman says "our failure has been not to Nagasaki them." Now there's some wang dang for you. If there's one thing about the Nuge, he is endlessly quotable. Here are his thoughts on people who refuse to carry handguns: "Don't wear any underpants and get raped. Cause you deserve it." Now that's not-so-sweet poontang.

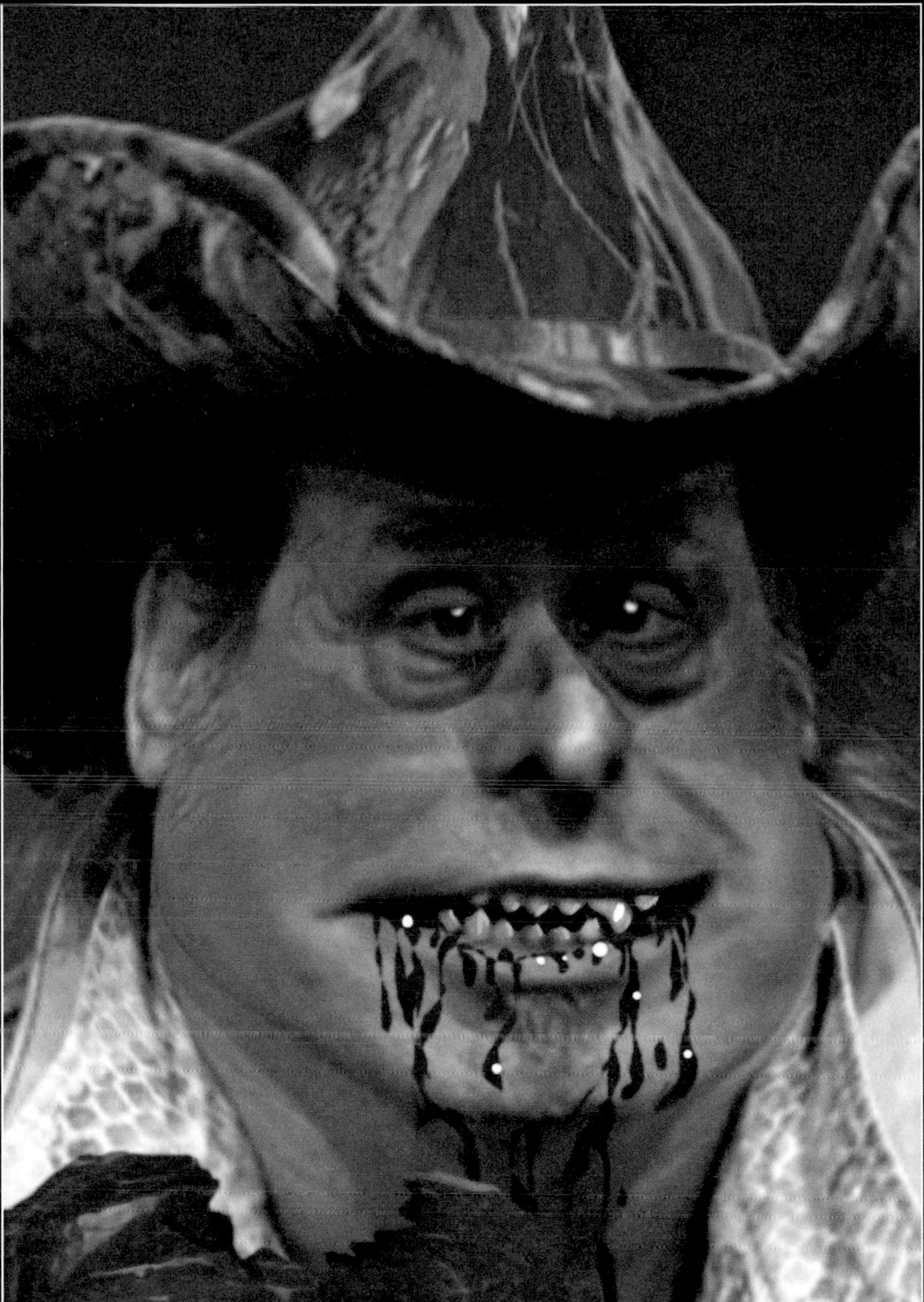

AFTER A SERIES OF FAKE controversies that O'Reilly tried to stir up, like the infamous "War on Christmas," he was feeling a little down in the dumps. People everywhere were still saying "Happy Holidays" instead of "Happy Birthday to the Glory that is Christ Our Lord and Savior Who Died for Your Sins. Would You Like that Gift-Wrapped?" Then, he struck gold. After four years of repeatedly calling abortion doctor Dr. George Tiller "Tiller the Baby Killer," O'Reilly scored a huge success when, in May of 2009, Tiller was murdered outside of his own church by one of O'Reilly's "Super Fans." Many would say that O'Reilly is not responsible for Tiller's death, but they are mostly lawyers for Fox News. O'Reilly came to prominence on a sleazy tabloid show called "Inside Edition," which is so rarely seen that no one might think to cancel it because they don't realize it's still on the air. He gets regular botulism infusions to build up enough crazy to rant on Fox News; this has had the convenient consequence of transforming his face into a site that can double as a toxic waste dump.

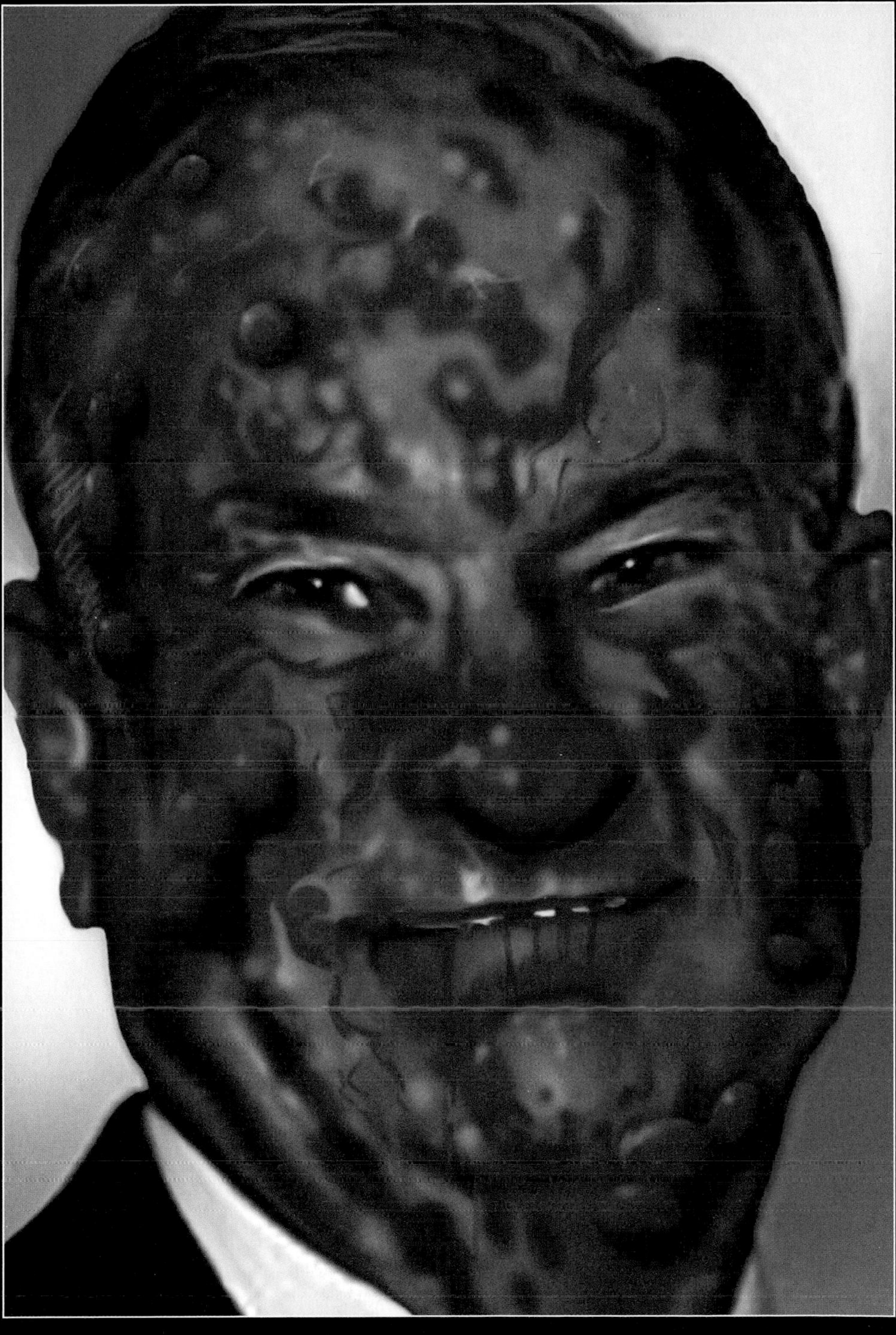

SHE QUIT HER JOB as Governor of Alaska because it took time away from her real job: being Sarah. The pay is phenomenal, you make your own hours, you can't get fired, and you can take your kids to work. And put them to work. So what if it's a little messy when a future *Playgirl* model knocks one of 'em up; the opportunities are endless. If anybody on the planet makes a sex joke or uses the word "retarded," you organize a protest, then you can get in the news and the checks roll in. C'mon, she didn't just waltz in from the oil-drenched tundra, where she was presumably hunting wolves from a helicopter, and saunter off to an all-expense-paid shopping spree at Neiman-Marcus yesterday. Although she has no experience in formulating national policy, and barely any experience formulating a sentence, she knows how to milk an applause line. Nasty one-liners delivered with a wink and a French manicure to the jugular was all she needed to convince 47% of voters she ought to be the Vice President of the United States of America. Her secret appeal? Obviously, a spell cast by her witch doctor.

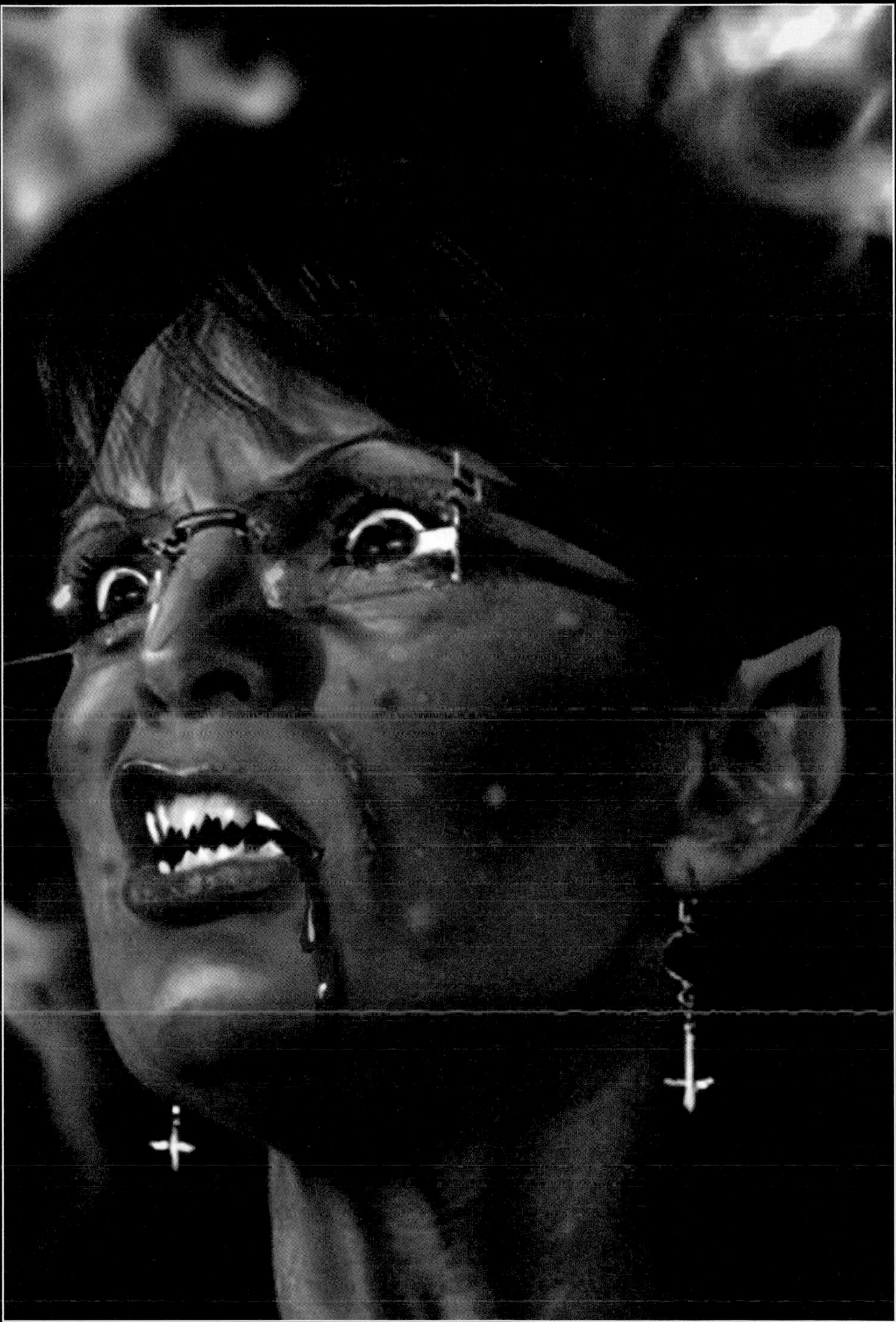

THIS HAR'S TEXAS and we're a pert stubborn lot. We don' like wut them fancy Harvard types and them's black president is doin' to our country. They's taking all our money and givin' it to queers and poor illegal aliens and pro'ly sum real aliens, too. Cuz I seen aliens, which is why I wears me a tinfoil hat to keep them frum beamin' crazy thowts dir'cly into ma brain. Next they's a gonna be a comin' fer our guns. Just you watch and I'll be a sayin' I told ya so. So's as gov'nur of this great state, I invite all y'all Teabagger super-patriot great Amercans to hoop 'n' holler it up so's we can tell them boys 'n' li'l gals in D.C. that we's had enuff o' this taxin' and such. If'n they keep it up we's gonna secede from the union an' make our own country jus like the pilgrims did. When us'n Texans joined the union in 1845 we sure enuf said we could always pull out. And my momma always told me pullin' out sometimes can save you a heap o' trubelz. Remember that thar Alamo!

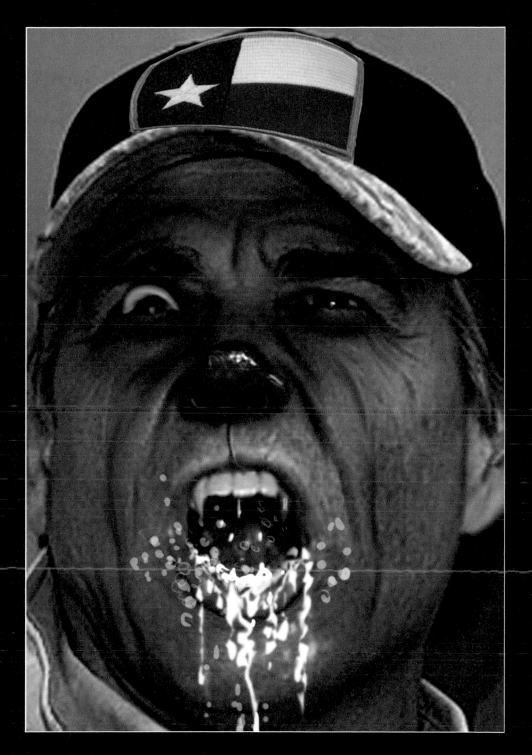

DEAR GOD,

Why did you send Pat Robertson and his big bag of crazy to earth to torment us? What did we do to deserve this "compassionate conservative" who thinks Hurricane Katrina was punishment for America's abortion policies, and the earthquake in Haiti was brought on because that nation made a pact with the devil? Was it reality TV, God? Is that our sin? Is that why you transmit messages through Pat like this gem: "I know this is painful for the ladies to hear, but if you get married, you have accepted the headship of a man, your husband. Christ is the head of the household and the husband is the head of the wife, and that's the way it is, period." Headship? I'd like a little more "headship" in my marriage, God, that's for sure. Lord, why did you tell Robertson to support George W. Bush for president even though Bush does not go to church? Bush says NOT going to church proves how religious he is because he doesn't need to prove anything. Is that okay, God? Because that's exactly what I say about a colonoscopy; not going to the proctologist proves how healthy I am.

Amen.

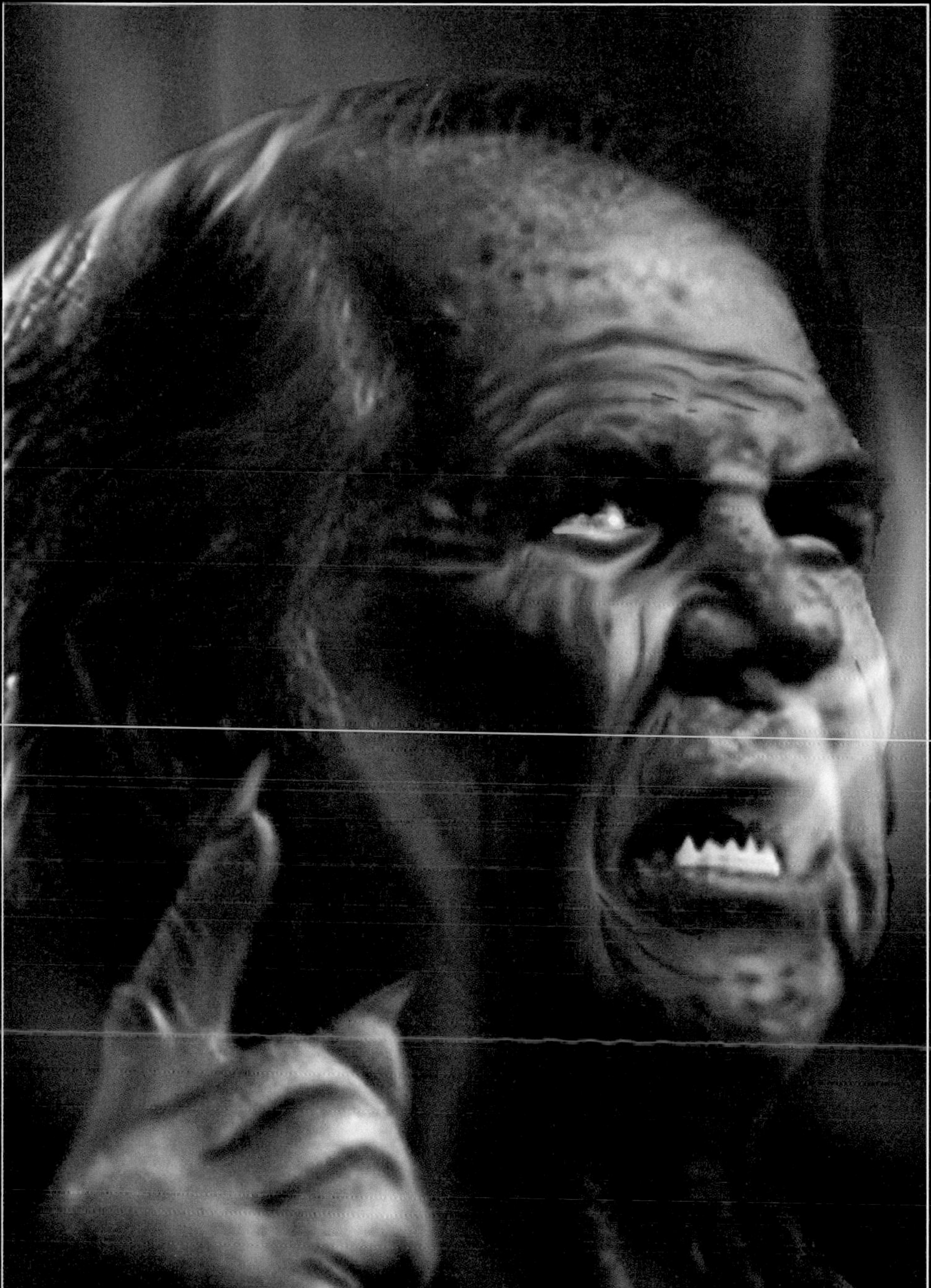

HE'S PUFFED-UP with his own importance but at least Mitt Romney has the best damn hair of any would-be president. Including Sarah Palin. John Edwards would give him a run for his money but it's unlikely he's running anytime soon. Mitt's hair actually has superpowers. It protects him from many things, but one thing it cannot protect him from is the fact that he's Mormon. America is ready for a black or woman president but not a Mormon. If America had to choose between a Mormon or gay president, color the White House fuchsia, sister. America doesn't want a Mormon president because, well, who wants to go to this party?

*The Presidential Committee*
*requests the honor of your presence at the*
*Inauguration of*

## Willard Mitt Romney

MODESTY OF DRESS AND MANNER STRICTLY ENFORCED
MEN: WHITE SHORT SLEEVE SHIRTS WITH TIE (NO JACKET)
WOMEN: DENIM JUMPERS AND SENSIBLE SHOES
NO SKIN SHOWING. NO MAKE-UP.
MAGICAL UNDERWEAR ESSENTIAL

ENTERTAINMENT:
THE OSMONDS
DAVID ARCHULETA
MORMON TABERNACLE CHOIR

DINNER SERVED FOLLOWED BY GREEN JELL-O
NO ALCOHOL, SODAS, COFFEE OR TEA.

CHILDREN WELCOME—THE MORE THE MERRIER.
SPOUSES WELCOME—DITTO.

R S V P

*Pray. We'll know.*

YOU MAY ALSO RSVP FOR THE DEAD.

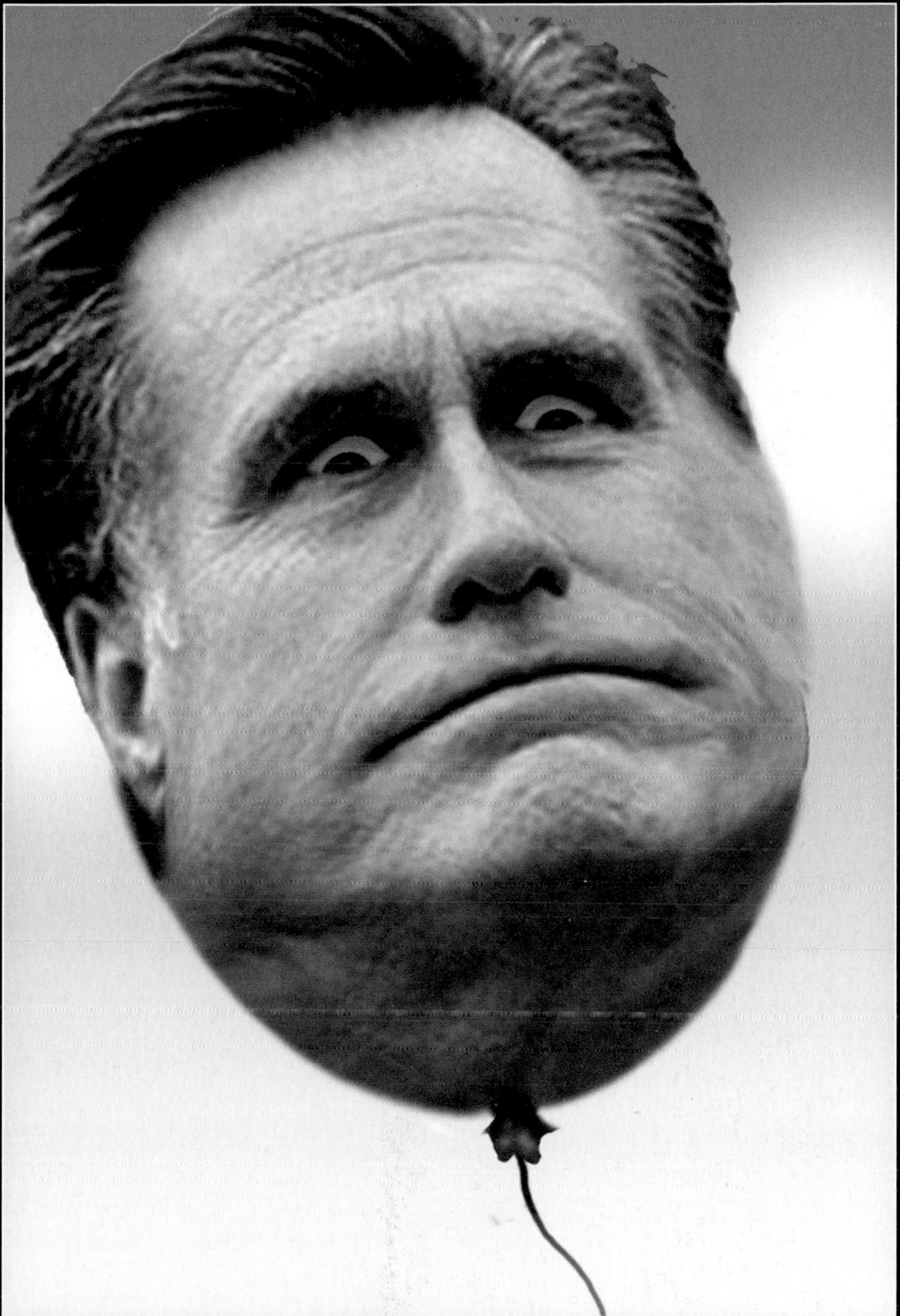

A DIRTY TRICKSTER PRODIGY. 19-year-old Karl Rove, in June of 1970, was already breaking into campaign offices and stealing stuff to undermine the opposition. A few years later, George Bush Sr. had the FBI question Rove because of his reputation for employing dirty tricks. Luckily, Bush Jr. was there to hire him specifically for his political "gifts." Karl (whom Junior nicknamed "Turd Blossom") then perfected the "push" poll; not really a poll at all, but instead a way to spread rumors to voters over the phone. Some of Karl's favorite push poll questions were along the lines of, "If you knew Governor Ann Richards was a lesbian, would it affect your decision to vote for her?" and "If you knew John McCain had fathered a black baby, would it affect your decision to vote for him?" Now, let's try one of our own: "If you knew Karl Rove was a radioactive zombie who had divorced his wife in December of 2009 to hook up with a gay male prostitute he had often entertained in the White House, would it make you think of him as a hypocrite?"

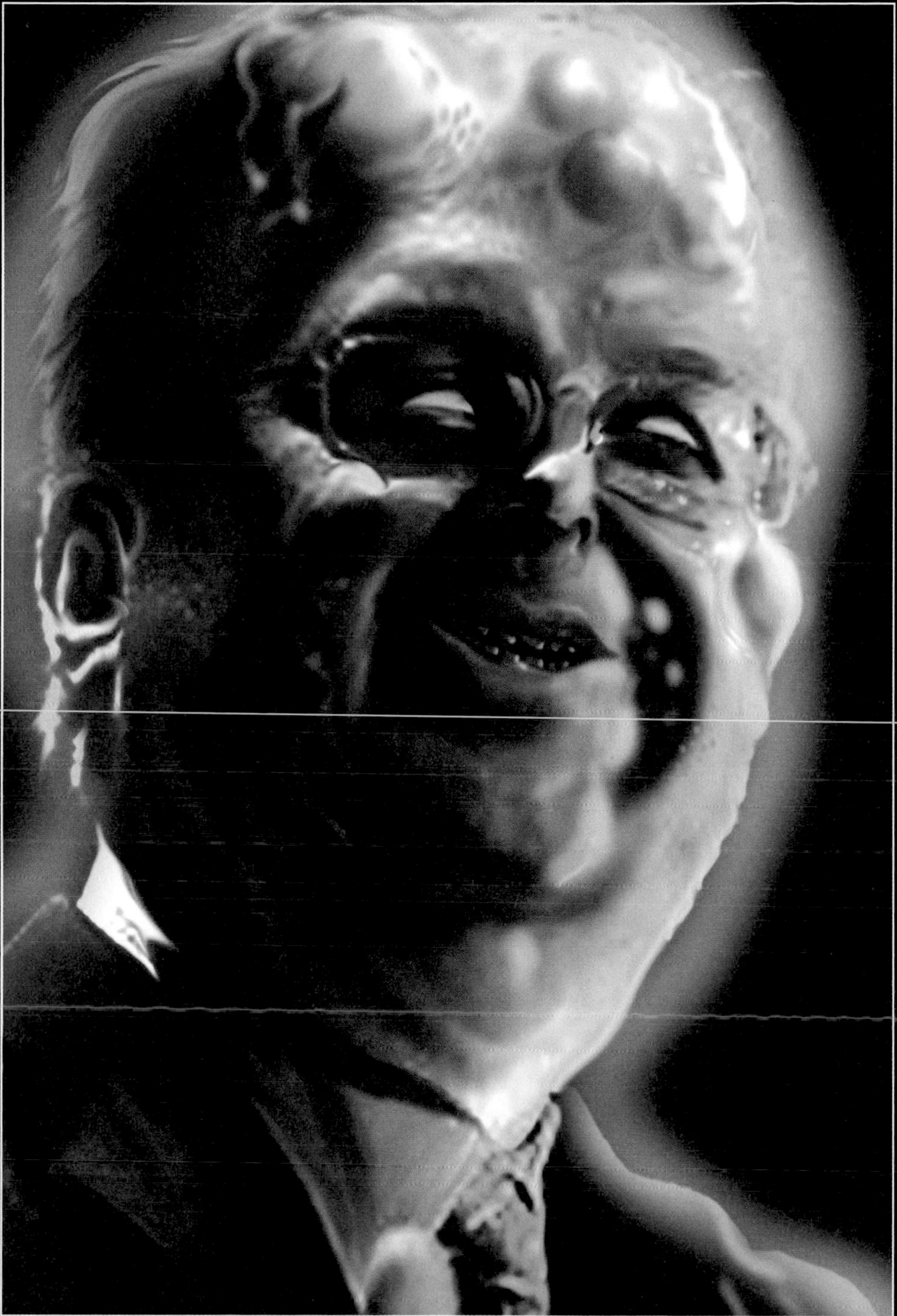

AFTER THE GREAT American abolitionist and reformer Frederick Douglass ran away from his former master in 1850, he was captured and tortured by "slave breaker" William Covey in a plantation in Maryland. Because of the unspeakable torture that routinely took place in that house, it was named "Mount Misery." Now it's a private home. Who could sleep at night among those memories? Donald Rumsfeld lives there today. Perhaps this is where he drew the inspiration for the torture of Iraqi prisoners at Abu Ghraib. As Secretary of Defense during the U.S. war in Iraq, he inspired many generals. In unprecedented numbers, he inspired them to call for his resignation. He worked for Presidents Nixon, Ford, Bush I and II. If he is so inept, how does he keep getting rehired? Simple, as Richard Nixon pointed out, he's a "ruthless little bastard." And that's coming from someone qualified to assess. This leader of the neo-cons is a force to be reckoned with. You see, he can shoot death rays from his eyes. It puts people in a hypnotic trance and they'll do whatever he says. And if someone disobeys, the rays can incinerate a full-grown man in seven seconds.

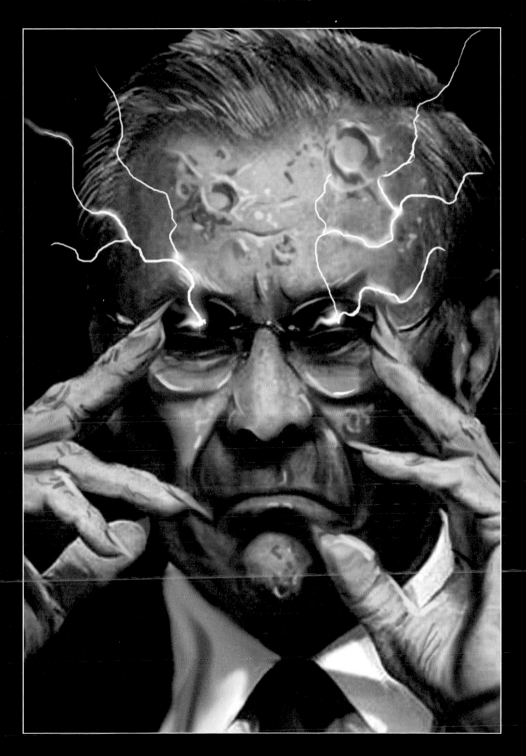

## THE MARK SANFORD QUIZ

### As a congressman, Sanford voted:

A) To impeach Clinton for his reprehensible behavior with
   Monica Lewinsky

B) Against issuing a breast cancer postage stamp

C) Against funding preservation of sites linked to the
   Underground Railroad

### As governor, Sanford:

A) Said his own reprehensible behavior shouldn't be cause for
   impeachment

B) Supported many women's breasts

C) Made voters want to railroad him outta town

### Sanford's number one priority as South Carolina's Governor was:

A) Foreign affairs

B) Searching for Appalachian Tail

C) Clearly he hasn't thought this whole thing through

### As a role model to his four sons, Sanford has shown how he:

A) Cheats on their mother

B) Publicly cries like a baby

C) Teaches them to do as I say, not whom I do

### What does Sanford like best about Argentina?:

A) Tapas

B) Topless

C) You can live it up at the taxpayers' expense

### Mark Sanford's wife's memoirs are called:

A) *Staying True*

B) *This'll Cost Ya*

C) *I'm Gonna Cut off Your Testicles with a Dull Butter Knife*

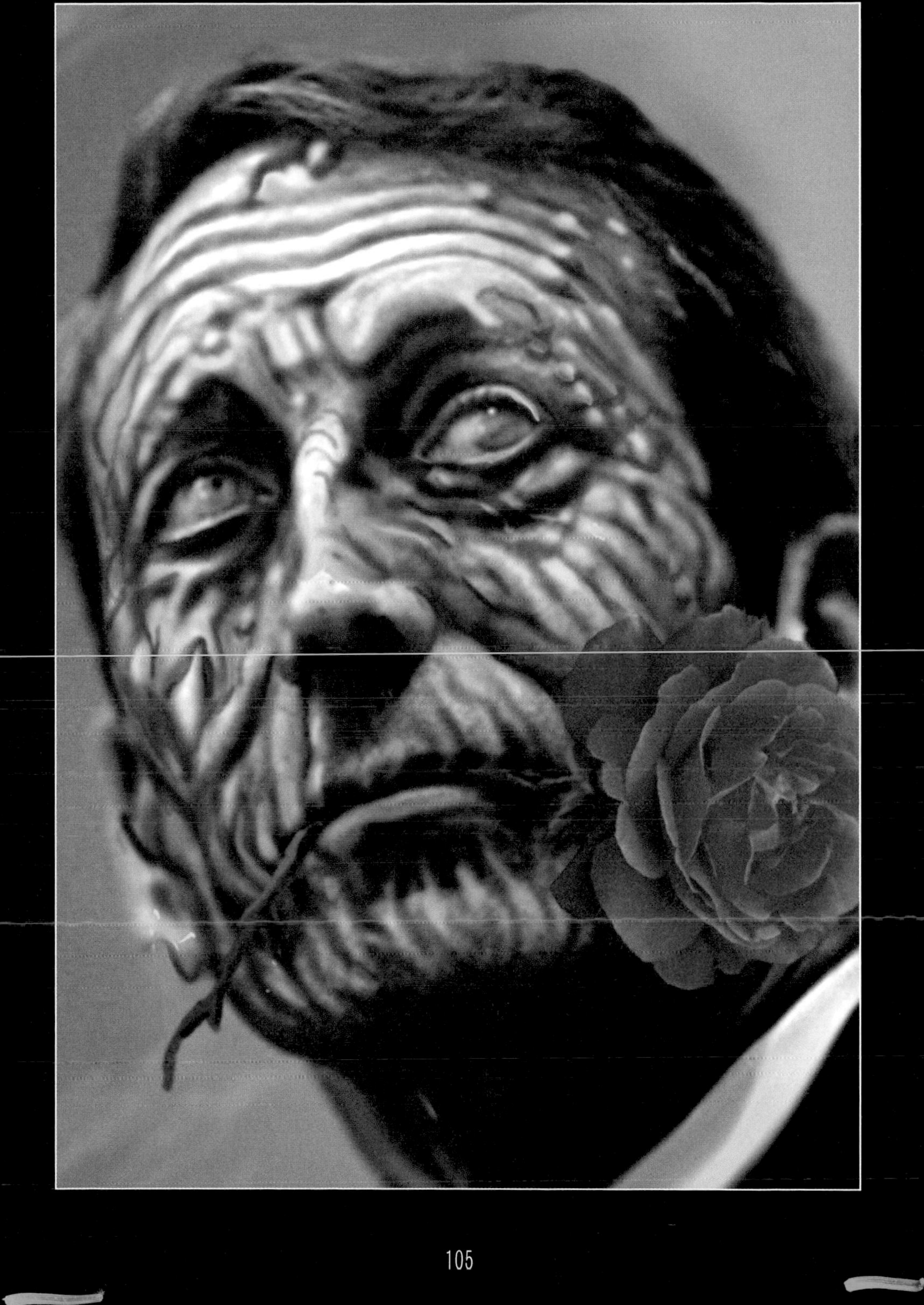

"IMPEACHMENT, MY PRECIOUS!" This billionaire Nixon fan and anti-government jihadist's dogged obsession with Bill Clinton was realized in his "Arkansas Project," a series of operations that included lying, threatening, disseminating misinformation, and generally trying to end the Clinton presidency. Everyone needs a hobby. This trust-fund baby had a lot of free time on his hands and few productive activities to fill it. Former Scaife employee Pat Minarcin said, "He has the emotional maturity of a very angry 12-year-old, and he has all this money and he can do whatever he wants with it." He used newspapers and think tanks like The Heritage Foundation to spread his crackpot theories. His employees wrote books like *The Strange Death of Vince Foster*, which even nutty right-wing publication *The American Spectator* said sounded like it was written by a "right-wing nut." The Billion Dollar Baby was running the Vast Right Wing Conspiracy out of his back porch and found a willing accomplice in one cigarette-lawyer-turned-prosecutor Ken Starr, who was eager to be a part of bringing down the White House. It almost worked, too. Wouldn't that have been precious?

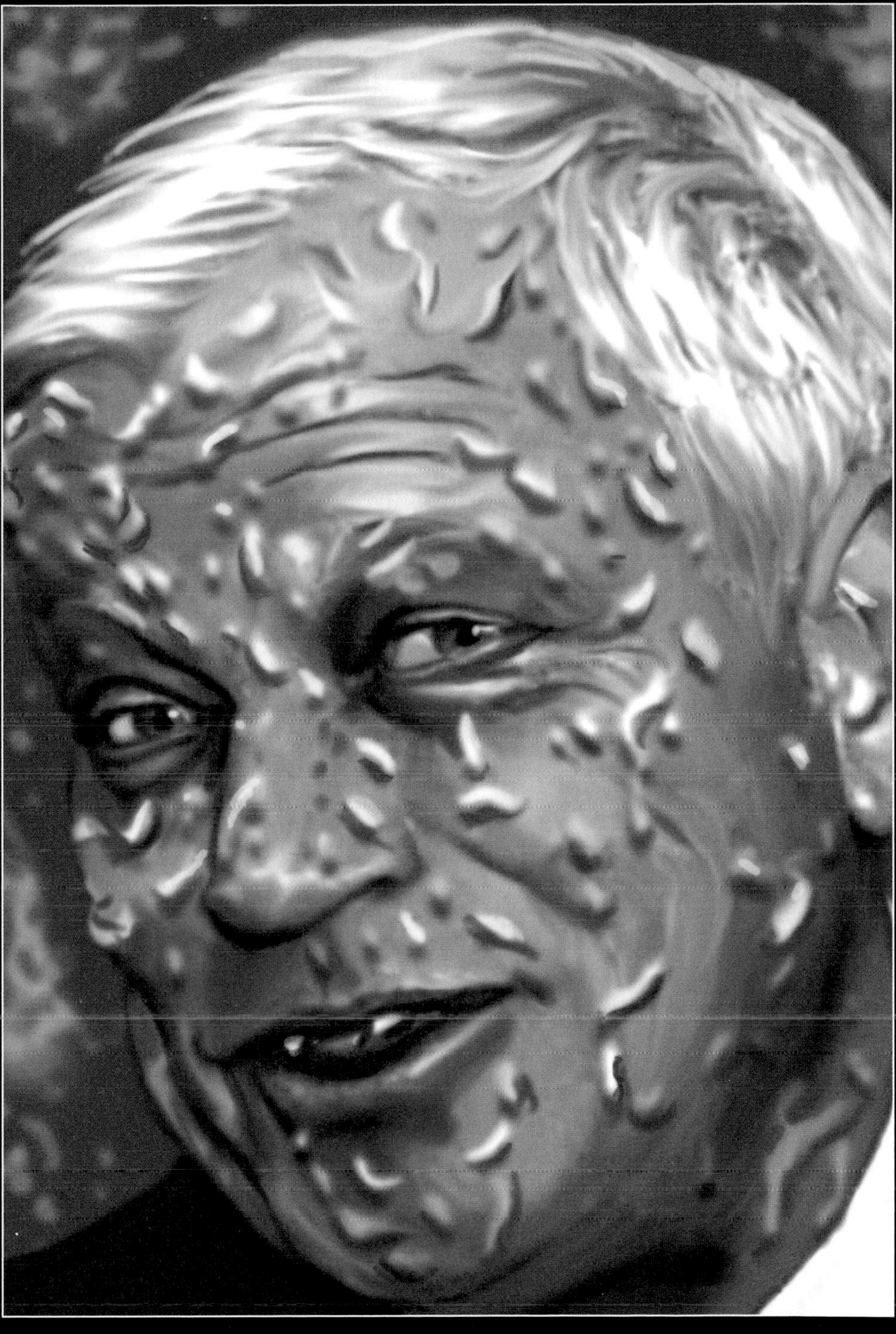

JUSTICE SCALIA has always been a reliable conservative vote in the way you'll reliably get an STD if you frequent certain unsavory places. When Repuglican henchman got the disputed presidential election of 2000 wrangled into the court, Scalia became a kingmaker. Since his son Eugene was a lawyer for Bush and on the case before the Florida Court, recusal might have been one way for Scalia to go. He went another way, and father and son tag-teamed Bush right into the White House. Criticism doesn't deter him. To illustrate the point, this evidence is entered into the record: during Lent of 2006, a Boston Herald reporter tracked down the Justice (who had just taken the Eucharist at the Cathedral of the Holy Cross) and tried to interview him. The judge gave a curt response. Scalia said "To my critics, I say, 'Vaffanculo!" which translates from the Italian to something like, "go get fucked up your ass." But really, who could defend the vote on *Bush vs. Gore*? To further clarify his opinion, the freshly absolved-from-sin judge then flicked his fingers under his chin in a gesture that means roughly the same thing. So much for judicial restraint.

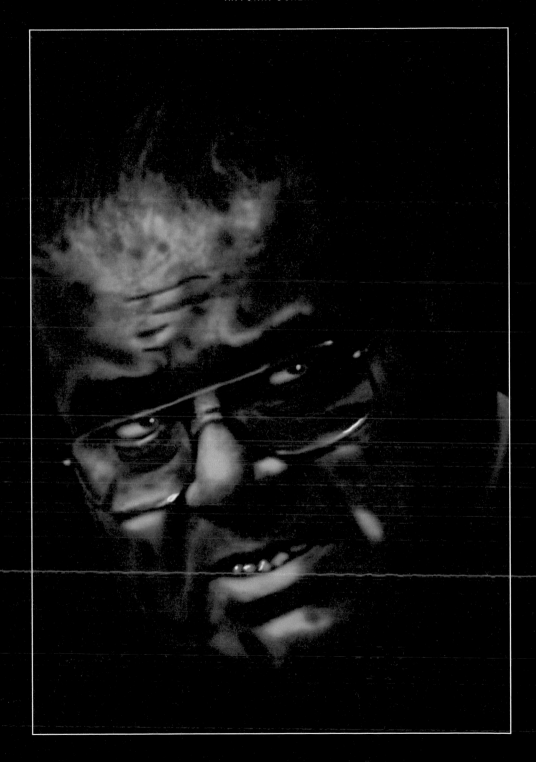

THIS LIVING CORPSE of America's shameful past said that the National Association for the Advancement of Colored People (NAACP) and the American Civil Liberties Union (ACLU) are "un-American" and "Communist-inspired" because they "forced civil rights down the throats of people." Yes, because as everyone knows, people hate to be forced to have rights. Senator Whitey thought the Ku Klux Klan was okay until, as he says, "I found out they smoked pot." Yes, because racism requires a clear head. He called a black attorney and colleague "boy." Sure, he admits saying it, but insists it was a "joke." He's a hilarious guy. Here are some other "jokes" he might want to try on for size: he might want to call himself a "jackass" or "douchebag" or something similarly knee-slapping. So how did President Bush repudiate this embarrassment? He campaigned for him for United States Senator from Alabama, natch. But, lest you think Sessions is limited, racism isn't his only passion; he's also pro-torture. Voting with a lonely minority to allow the US to engage in practices unacceptable according to the Geneva Convention, he sealed his fate as one of the most out of touch of Repuglicans.

# JEFFERSON BEAUREGARD "JEFF" SESSIONS III

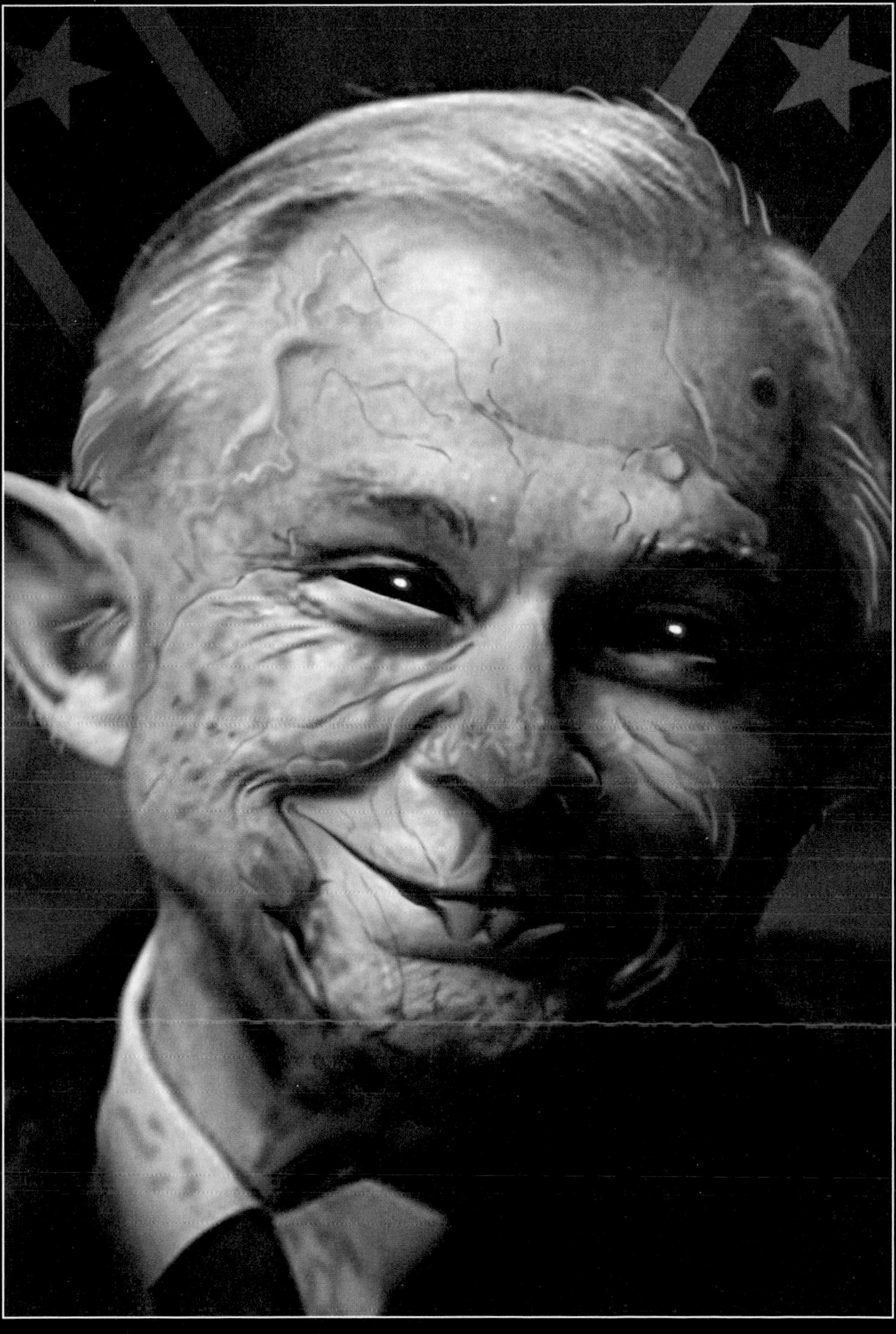

YOU MIGHT BE STARTLED to discover this, but there are limits to how much politicians can cheat and lie. Sometimes, they have to call someone to do it for them. And that someone is Craig Shirley. He was the publicist who made Paula Jones into a famed Clinton accuser and *Penthouse* model. He was the guy who made former FBI agent Gary Aldrich a lot of money promoting Aldrich's tall-tale, "tell-all" book about the Clintons. He was the guy who worked for George W. Bush in 2000, spreading rumors about Al Gore. And he was the one who said that campaign consultants like himself are "here forever. They take over. They're like cockroaches that come out in the middle of the night." Of his many Hall of Fame-worthy fabrications, perhaps his proudest moment was when he took the story of Pfc. Jessica Lynch, who never fired a shot and was in fact unconscious when she was taken prisoner in Iraq in 2003, and helped make her into a larger-than-life G.I. Jane, though he knew his story contained not a shred of truth. Everyone needs a hero and to the Repuglicans, that hero is Craig Shirley.

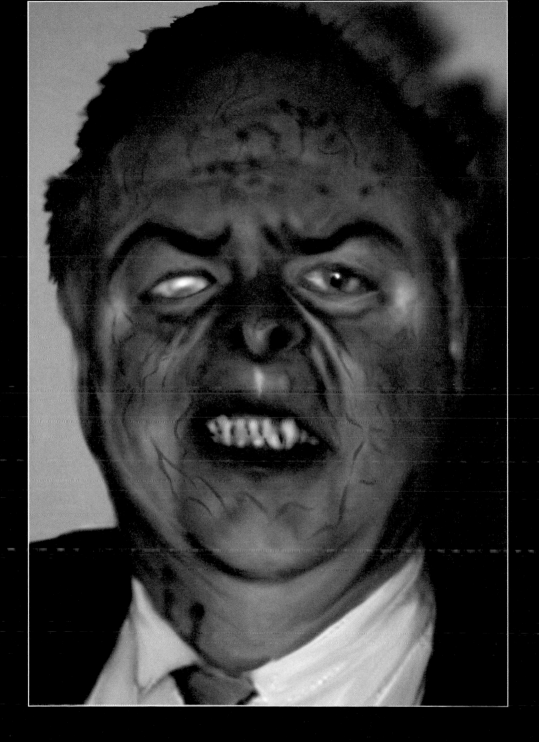

THE REPUBLICANS LIKE TO CLAIM that they're a Big Tent party. Unfortunately for them, when you look at how they are aging, they'll need an oxygen tent. They are losing their grip on younger voters, Hispanic voters, and black voters. So, in a cynical Hail Mary pass in the era of Obama, they dredged the depths of their NASCAR-loving membership and came up with the one black dude willing to take the reins of party leadership. Hello Michael Steele! Did it work? With stellar credentials like being Mike Tyson's brother-in-law, what could go wrong? The disastrous results of his tenure speak for themselves. When he took on the role as head of the party (in name only, of course, as we all know Rush Limbaugh is the real head of the party), it was in disarray and about as popular as Roman Polanski at a "Mommy and Me" class, and things have gone steadily downhill from there.

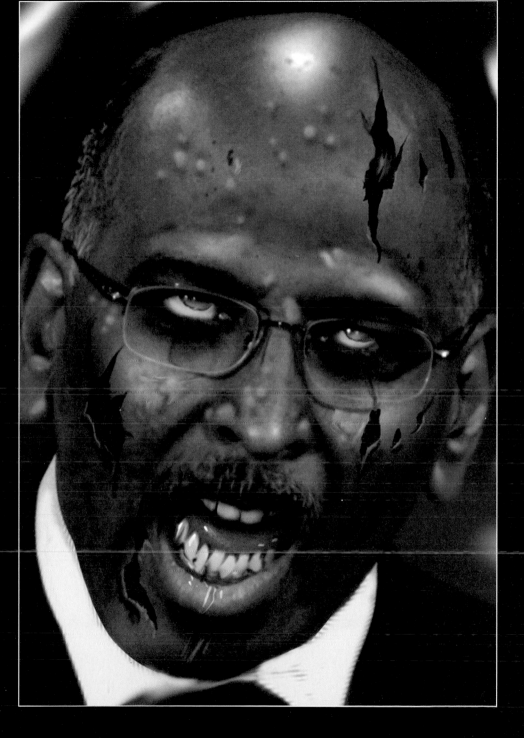

BEN STEIN loves Richard Nixon's legacy so much that, I kid you not, he actually has a condo in the Watergate building. As only a former lawyer for Richard Nixon could argue, Mr. Stein asserts that all who exposed the misdeeds in the Nixon White House are responsible for genocide, because if Nixon had been allowed to serve out his term, committing whatever felonies and betrayals of the American public he deemed fit, he most certainly would have stopped the Khmer Rouge. Does anyone buy this argument? Anyone? Anyone? Bueller? Well, Mr. Stein, maybe if we had let him commit more crimes, he would have cured cancer. Just about all of Stein's crazy hit parade of theories have something to do with genocide. He's even made *Expelled*, a "documentary" film in which he argued that the theory of evolution led to genocide. He also said in an interview on the Trinity Broadcasting Network (yes, the one featuring that lady with the crazy wigs) that, while God leads you to a glorious place, "science leads you to killing people." Of course it does, everyone knows that. Luckily, religion has never led anybody to kill people. Oh wait! Never mind.

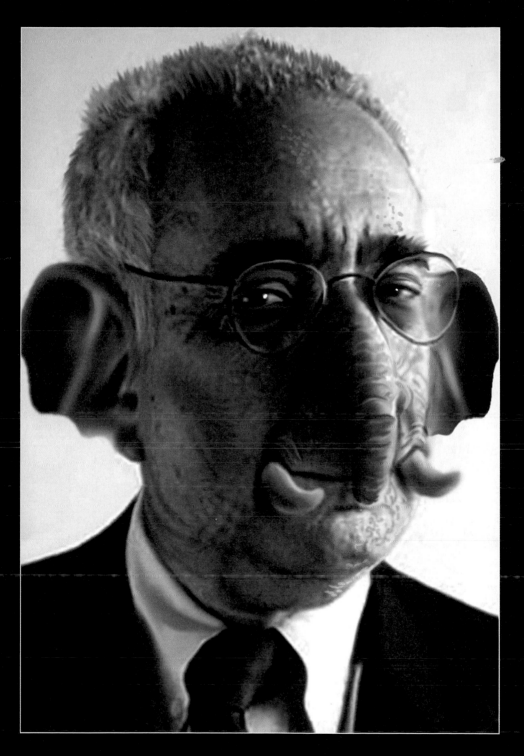

IF YOU WAKE UP NEXT TO HER after a long night in a bar, just put a gun in your mouth, because she's never going to get over it. She will not be ignored! Orly Taitz is an Orange County dentist with a law degree she picked up on the Internet and an Eva Gabor wig she picked up at a Zody's close-out sale. This disturbed creature has found her purpose as the leader of the Birthers, a group of foaming-at-the-mouth lunatics who claim to believe that President Obama is not a natural-born American citizen, despite the fact that anyone with a dial-up modem and a spare 20 seconds can prove their accusations false. But she persists in leading her troops in filing frivolous lawsuits, undaunted by the threat of disbarment. This woman owns more bad suits than have ever hung in Janet Reno's closet. Though her followers are few, they are chock full o' nuts. Among Orly's like-minded adherents is Minister Wiley Drake, who was presidential candidate Alan Keyes' running mate on the America's Independent Party 2008 ticket. Minister Drake has, in the past, called Barack Obama an "illegal alien" and has publicly prayed for his death. That's right, Who Would Jesus Kill?

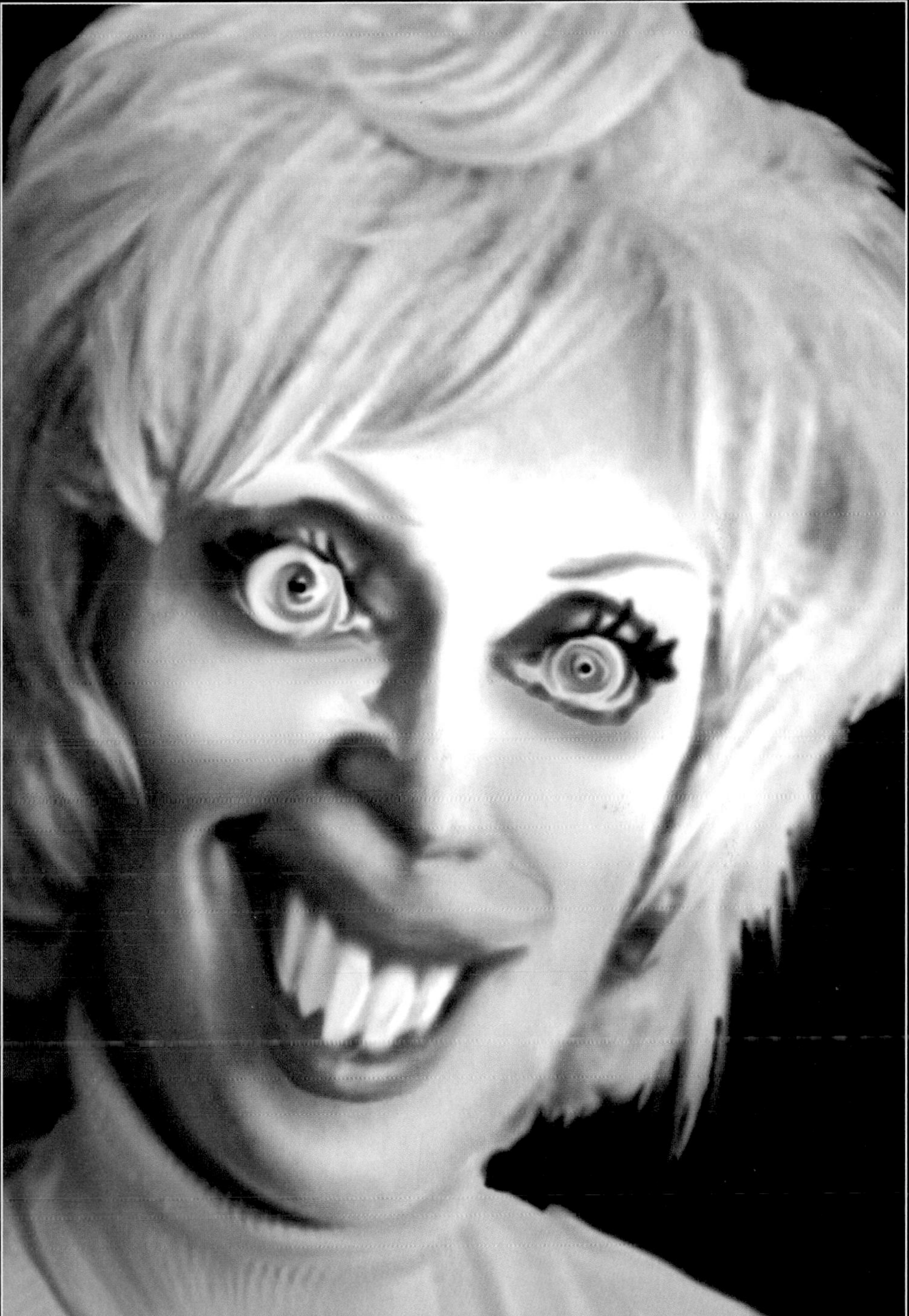

FORMER COLORADO CONGRESSMAN Tom Tancredo's blood runs so cold that he said illegal immigrants "need to be found before it is too late. They're coming here to kill you, and you, and me, and my grandchildren." Which I guess is just Tom's way of saying, "Give me your tired, your poor, your huddled masses yearning to breathe free." While running for President, he accused Pope Benedict XVI of encouraging illegal immigration to the United States in order to increase membership in the Catholic Church, saying, "I suspect the Pope's immigration comments may have less to do with spreading the gospel than they do about recruiting new members of the church." New members? I thought that was what the free wine was for. While on CNN, he called Supreme Court Justice nominee Sonya Sotomayor a racist and said that the Hispanic-American advocacy group La Raza is the "KKK without the hoods." He's not only about the immigration. He has other issues. He's in favor of legalizing marijuana and apparently partakes prior to giving interviews on CNN.

A "TEABAGGER" is someone who dunks his testicles into another person's mouth. It's super-hilarious that Mark Williams and his band of right-wing crazies are regularly called this in countless respectable publications. Williams provides inspirational leadership for the Teabaggers, AKA Tea Partyers, by doing things like calling Jimmy Carter a "faggot" on his blog, which at least he spelled right, in stark contrast to the illiterate placards held up at many of the Teabagger rallies. Williams' group doesn't like taxes and they're not so crazy about the U.S. government either, so they named themselves after the Boston Tea Party. The problem is, the Boston Tea Party was held in 1773 because Americans were fighting for their RIGHT to be TAXED by their own ELECTED REPRESENTATIVES. So Williams has history perfectly right, except exactly the opposite. The Teabaggers' biggest beef is against big government, which they love to call "socialism." By the way, 100% of the time when they are holding rallies against so-called socialism, they are gathered on public land, protected by collectively-paid-for public police, underneath the lights of public utilities. Socialism completes them. Alanis Morissette could sing a song about it.

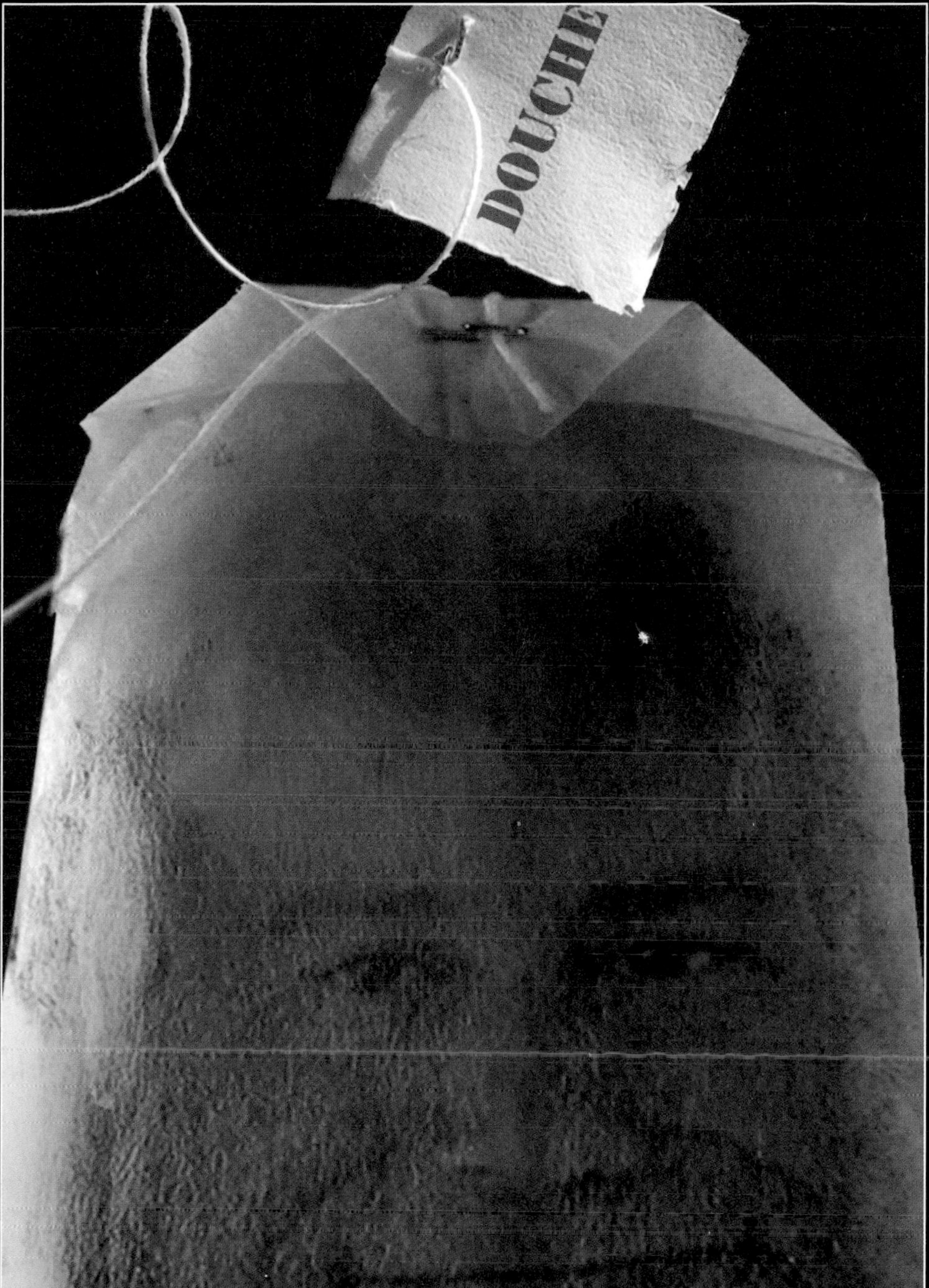
DOUCHE

DEAR ABBY,

I recently attended a dignified event where I sat amongst prominent national leaders. It was a joint session of Congress, and I was there to listen to a presidential address; an American tradition reaching back to 1789. As an elected representative of my district in South Carolina, I knew families would be watching proudly, witnessing their government in action. When the president, from the podium, outlined a proposed piece of legislation, I decided to scream out "You lie!", even though what the president said was factually correct. Just because. It reminded me of the time I was on C-SPAN with Bob Filner and I blurted out that he was making stuff up, even though I kinda knew what he was saying was true. Well, anyway, after my outburst, checks started rolling into my reelection campaign. I got $2.5 million in donations! If I had known it was so easy to get people's money, I would have tried this years ago. So I'm thinking of attending famous people's funerals and yelling "You die!" Or maybe going to public executions and screaming "You fry!" My question is: which do you think would be more profitable?

Signed Me,
Big Mouthed Joe

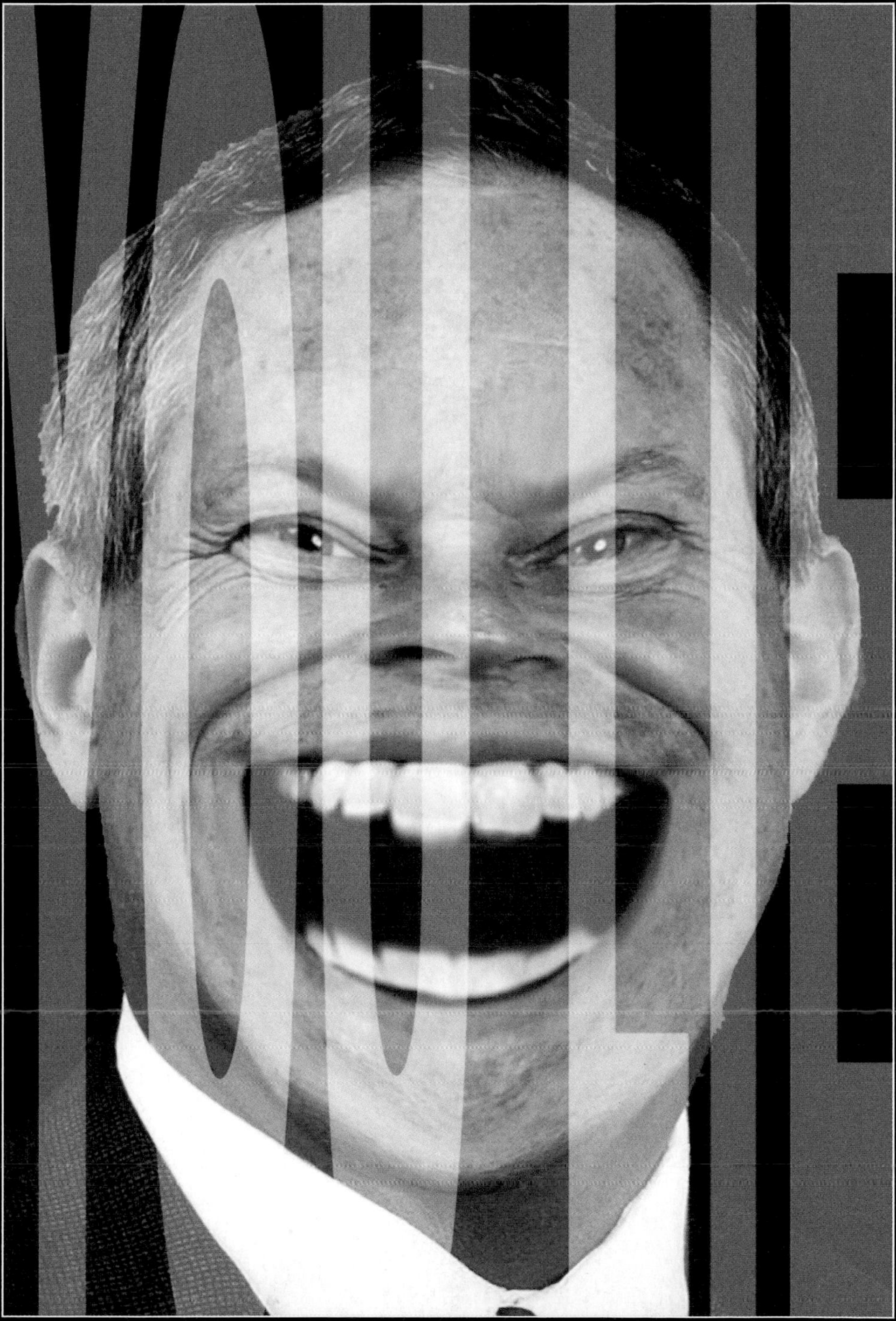
YOU LIE

Born in New York, PETE VON SHOLLY has storyboarded over 100 feature films including *The Shawshank Redemption, Mars Attacks!, Darkman, James and the Giant Peach, The Green Mile* and *The Mist.* Dark Horse Publishing has published three of Von Sholly's critically acclaimed graphic novels entitled *Morbid, Morbid 2: Dead but Not Out!* and *Extremely Weird Stories.* Von Sholly's work has also been seen in his satiric magazines from TwoMorrows Publishing, *Comic Book Nerd* and *Crazy Hip Groovy Go-Go Way-Out Monster*s, as well as Last Gasp's *Forbidden Knowledge* and *Neurocomics,* which he did with Timothy Leary. For those who would prefer a bi-partisan take on political horror please see Von Sholly's *Capitol Hell* book from Denis Kitchen Publishing.

STEVE TATHAM is the author of *1001: A Video Odyssey, Movies to Watch for Your Every Mood.* He has performed stand-up comedy on TV, radio and in clubs around the country. Tatham wrote and performed 562 episodes of the online show "The Ointment" for which he was named one of *L.A. Weekly's People of 2008.* He lives in the Los Angeles area with his wife and two children and is a recovering Republican.